# ILLUMINATING THE PROPHECY

## About the Author

Maggie Stiefvater's life decisions have revolved around her inability to be gainfully employed. Talking to yourself, staring into space, and coming to work in your pajamas are frowned upon when you're a waitress, calligraphy instructor, or technical editor (all of which she's tried), but are highly prized traits in novelists and artists (she's made her living as one or the other since she was twenty-two). Maggie now lives a surprisingly eccentric life in the middle of nowhere, Virginia, with her charmingly straight-laced husband, two kids, and neurotic dog.

## To Write to the Author

If you wish to contact the author or would like more information about this book, please write to the author in care of Llewellyn Worldwide Ltd. and we will forward your request. Both the author and publisher appreciate hearing from you and learning of your enjoyment of this book and how it has helped you. Llewellyn Worldwide Ltd. cannot guarantee that every letter written to the author can be answered, but all will be forwarded. Please write to:

Maggie Stiefvater
% Llewellyn Worldwide
2143 Wooddale Drive
Woodbury, MN 55125-2989

Please enclose a self-addressed stamped envelope for reply, or $1.00 to cover costs. If outside the U.S.A., enclose an international postal reply coupon.

MAGGIE
STIEFVATER

# ILLUMINATING THE PROPHECY

Llewellyn Publications
Woodbury, Minnesota

First Edition
Seventh Printing, 2021


Cover design by Lisa Novak
Interior art on page 15 by the Llewellyn Art Department



ISBN 978-0-7387-4743-9
The Raven's Prophecy Tarot kit consists of a boxed set of 78 full-color cards and this perfect-bound book.



Llewellyn Publications
A Division of Llewellyn Worldwide Ltd.
2143 Wooddale Drive
Woodbury, MN 55125-2989
www.llewellyn.com

# CONTENTS

# 1

# INTRODUCTION

I love stories.

I love them in all forms: in writing, in art, in music. I love how humans everywhere feel compelled to fold and carve and structure events into a narrative—we've been doing it for as long as we've been around. We mutter cautionary tales to remind others what frightens us, whisper love stories to give form to our hope, and shout heroic epics to underline what we believe in. My favorite sorts of stories, however, are the ones that people tell about themselves.

To me, that's the soul of tarot. Every spread is an opportunity to shape our current life events into a story with ourselves firmly installed as the hero at the heart of it. Stories are a way of imposing structure and control, and tarot is a way of imposing structure and control on our own spiritual growth. Tarot is inherently self-centered, helping you understand what *you* can control in your current situation, even if you feel powerless. It's also inherently positive: even the most negative cards in the deck are ultimately focused on emotional health and becoming a better version of yourself. It's also inherently intimate. The cards are not magic. The wisdom in them is really just the wisdom in you.

When I first started looking into tarot, I was daunted by the sheer amount of information I needed to tackle. Seventy-eight card meanings to memorize, countless spreads to learn, and endless terminology to internalize. My early attempts to read the cards were pitifully unsuccessful. I followed all the steps. I read the first card. Then I checked my books and read the second. Then the third. Rinse and repeat. It was very perfunctory. I suppose I thought reading tarot cards was like ... building a deck. Look up a plan, follow the steps, enjoy an ice-cold glass of tea on an elevated patio you constructed yourself. Cheers. Cheers!

It didn't work. I never got to that glass of iced tea. I just had a table full of random cards.

It wasn't until I had my cards read by two of my writer friends that I started to realize how personal the cards could be. How fluid the meanings were. How they interacted. How creative it all was, really. It had never been about reading this card, then another, then another. It was about learning to take them all together, to allow their interpretations to fit into each other like puzzle pieces, to make them a *story*. As an artist, I should have known better: there are no check boxes in art.

Tarot is at its best when it becomes absolutely intuitive.

Ultimately, you should glance at a spread and see a story about you. A wise mirror.

In this brief book, I'll cover the basics that you need to get started with tarot. Each card description will provide keywords to help you remember the core meaning of the card, and a fuller description that includes why I chose the image I did for the card. My hope is to help someone new to tarot to internalize the meanings as quickly and easily as possible, so that it stops being deck-building and starts being story-making. Because that's when it gets interesting.

Let's begin at the beginning.

# 2

# ABOUT THE THEME

This deck began because of a story.

I was writing a series that reveled in Welsh mythology and involved tarot, and what started as a gentle dabble in combining the two as a visual extra for readers exploded quite naturally into me drawing the entire deck. I was shocked to discover that the challenge of illustrating tarot was not dissimilar to writing a novel. Each piece of art was an agreeable puzzle. An opportunity to illustrate a succinct metaphor, to create a visual shortcut for the meaning of the card. I also found that the imagery of Welsh mythology paired beautifully with traditional tarot visuals. I borrowed the curious and cunning Welsh ravens to symbolize our logical, conscious minds and emphasized the traditional fire of the wands suit to represent creative force throughout the entire deck.

It took no time at all before it became a deck about being an artist.

I'm biased, of course. As a storyteller, a musician, and an artist, the push-pull relationship between logic and creativity has always fascinated me. So much of tarot is about balancing opposing forces in your life; it only took a bit of a nudge to make it about balancing our creative and logical selves. Only a bit of a nudge to make it about me. What can I say? We all like stories about ourselves.

I think it will work out. We're all of us artists in one way or another.

# 3

# HOW TO DO A READING

*Story, story*—I keep saying *story.* I'm going to say it again. A reading is a story.

A reading is also a ritual; it's about *intention.* About asking a question and genuinely wanting to know the answer. About being sure about the meaning of each position in your spread. About believing that you will discover *some* sort of insight through the process, even if it is not what you want to hear. Eventually, you'll devise your own method that feels true, but you'll only find it through a method of trial and error. Ultimately, you start by just picking a spread and feeling it out.

The most basic of readings merely involves selecting a single card from the deck and applying the meaning of the card to your current situation.

Simple, right? Simple, right.

Sometimes simple is all I need, but most of the time, I find my questions require a bit more nuance to answer. More nuance means more cards. That also means I need to understand how the positions of a tarot spread affect the meanings of the card, and how the cards affect each other. If you're new to tarot, I think you'd better take the deck out now. Put it in front of your face. Behold it. Do you have it? Good.

## Major Arcana

The first twenty-two cards are called the major arcana. These are often the cards that folks recognize from popular media. We've all seen countless movies where a mystical woman gasps as she produces the Death card (it doesn't mean death), or coos as she reveals the Lovers (which does not necessarily promise love—you just can't trust everything you see in the movies). Traditional wisdom often dictates that an overwhelming appearance of major arcana cards in a reading mean that it's going to be more significant than usual. Personally, I tend to think that all readings are significant. Every day is significant, which means every reading is a chance to change your life. The minor arcana have complex, specific meanings and without them, it can be difficult to figure out how to put into practice what the major arcana recommend.

## Minor Arcana

The rest of the cards (there are seventy-eight total) are called minor arcana, or pips. They're organized into four suits: cups, coins, swords, and wands. The cups suit is generally concerned with relationships and is associated with water. It's the *feels* suit. The coins suit is interested in material and physical things and is associated with earth. It's the bill-paying suit. The swords suit is interested in all things logical and argumentative and is associated with pain. No, no, I'm kidding. It's associated with air. It can be a difficult suit, which we'll get to later. And the wands suit—be still, my heart—is associated with creativity and fire. If a reading is dominated by one suit or another, it's a good indication that whatever that suit rules is dominating your thoughts just as equally. If you've asked a question about creativity and you've got a spread full of coins, it's a sign you might be thinking about financial or practical concerns instead of a budding art project.

## Court Cards

The court cards are the four cards that come at the end of each of the minor suits—the Page, the Knight, the Queen, and the King. Usually I read them as a person: a side of you that needs to be emphasized or de-emphasized, or a person in your life. This *living* quality can make them quite difficult to read; they're not like any of the other cards in the deck.

It can help to remember that they share some characteristics. Generally, the pages are full of youthful optimism, the knights represent an active extreme of whichever suit they are part of, the queens are maternal and experienced, and the kings represent a restrained master of their suit.

## Cycles

There are several cyclical journeys described in the tarot deck. The major arcana represents a journey that begins at the Fool and continues through experience to the World. Each of the minor suits likewise is a progressive cycle, one through ten, followed by the court cards, which are themselves a progression, with the King being more experienced than the Page. The placement of a card within the cycle will often tell you something about the meaning, and it's useful to learn these first, and add the nuance of each later. For instance, if you pulled the Two of Wands, even if you knew nothing about the nuanced meaning of the card, you could guess that it was about a creative project, because it was a wand, and you could guess that it was early in the endeavor or undeveloped, because it was only a Two. The Aces are always powerful beginnings in their respective suits; the Tens are always completion. Other patterns will appear the longer you've been reading.

## THE NITTY GRITTIES

These are the steps I take when I read:

1. Knock on the deck. I've always been told to have the querent (that's the person being read for) knock on the deck at the start of a reading to "knock the energy" of the last reading out. I like the ritual of it. It feels like I'm knocking at the door of wisdom: "I'm ready," it says.
2. Hold the deck to your heart and ask your question. I pray while I do this, because I'm a religious sort; your mileage may vary. I find a reading is most useful when I have a pointed question. Tarot is, after all, generally giving you answers that are already hiding inside you, and if you don't really know what you're looking for on some level, you'll end up with a muddled story that you can't understand the point of. Sometimes I ask questions about specific decisions in my life. Other times I will ask about projects I'm working on. One of my favorite questions to ask myself is, "What do I need to hear that I'm not listening to?" I'm good at making goals for myself and can easily mow over my intuition with a plausible sounding plan, and this is a way to get me to see outside of my practical-sounding plans.
3. Shuffle. I tell the folks I'm reading for to shuffle until they feel done. Sometimes a card will escape the deck while I shuffle, and I set that aside to read later—often it will provide clarification to the rest of the reading.

My sister, an intuitive creature, will sometimes pull a card out and say, "This card is what I want, but not what I need," and have me read it later.

4. Divide the deck into three piles. Pick the pile you like the best (sometimes it will feel warm or look... special), and restack the deck with that pile on top.
5. Lay out the cards. I lay them out face up; I want to see the story unfold.

The important thing to remember is what I said earlier: *tarot is about intention*. There are no specific rules, and if a step feels absolutely wrong or ridiculous to you, you can work your way towards a more personal method. It's also enlightening to have someone else read for you. You can pick up all kinds of tricks that way, or see something you already knew put into practice in a way that helps it make sense.

## Reversed Tarot Card Meanings

Some tarot readers read cards with slightly different meanings (often negative) if they appear upside down when laid out in the reading. I'm not going to go over reversed card meanings in this book; I find the cards carry all the nuance they need without complicating it even more with additional definitions to memorize.

# 4

# THE SPREADS

If you type "tarot spread" into any search engine, you will rapidly find yourself with more results than you can shake a stick at, if you are the sort to shake sticks at search results. A spread is merely a way of structuring and prioritizing the cards. They range from the very simple—a single card pulled after asking a question—to the very complex—a seventy-eight card spread detailing someone's entire life story. There's no such thing as a "best" spread.

I'm going to briefly go over the only three I ever use, but I suggest trying out several to see which seems most useful to you.

## The Single Card Reading

This is the simplest reading of all, and it's also the one I use the least. Usually, if I bother to do a reading for myself,

I'm facing some perplexing problem that is too complex for me to address with a single card. That said, sometimes if a problem is too huge to even tackle with a reading, I will sometimes pull a single card as a sort of weather report. I will follow the steps I outlined in the "How to Do a Reading" section and then I'll ask myself, *What's the situation?* and read a single card.

## The Three Card Reading

This is a slightly more elaborate reading, and I'll often do this if someone is at my house and asks for a reading while we're both pressed for time. I like this one best for very direct questions like, *Do I need a new job?* Or, *Should I break up with my useless boyfriend?*

Then I pull three cards:

1 – Past
2 – Present
3 – Future

The first card tells me the situation that led to the current question. The second card describes the nuances of the situation. The third card suggests a course of action or describes what the ideal outcome would be.

## The Ten-Card Reading

This spread was taught to me by a friend after she heard I was struggling with one of the most popular tarot spreads, the Celtic Cross. This spread is appropriate for nearly every

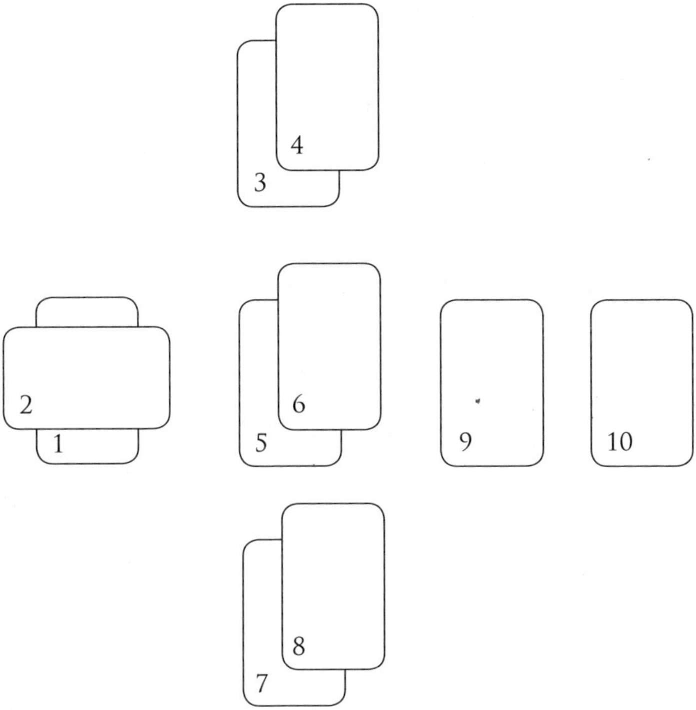


question I've ever tossed at the cards. Like I said previously, I often pose some variation of the question, *What do I need to hear that I'm not listening to?* The more nebulous your question, the more nebulous your answer, so I always try to be very specific with my intentions.

1. Self—your current mental situation or current defining external situation.
2. Crossed by—a complicating factor of the current self situation.

3. Unconscious—factor dominating your unconscious.
4. Conscious—factor dominating your waking thoughts.
5. What you think will help the situation—this is not necessarily wrong or right; it's only your perceived path.
6. What you think will hinder the situation—again, not necessarily wrong or right, merely your perceived path.
7. What will actually help—a real path out of the situation.
8. What will actually hinder—a path to avoid.
9. The path—the next step in the immediate future.
10. The outcome—what following the steps will lead you to.

# 5

# THE MAJOR ARCANA

It can be daunting to memorize the meanings of the tarot cards, especially when one realizes how nuanced the meanings of many of the cards are. At best, it's distracting to have to continually reference a booklet for the card meanings during a reading; at worst, it can keep you from seeing the overall story that a reading is trying to tell you.

The images on the cards are meant to jog your memory, and you'll quickly find that you begin to remember the cards you draw most often. I've tried to help out by providing a "cheat list" of keywords for each card, so even if you don't recall the more nuanced meaning, you can at least get a general idea of the story in front of you before you break open the book for reference.

Also, you'll find that the cards begin to take on more personal definitions the longer you've been reading tarot for yourself and for friends. Some cards will always remind me of some family members, for instance, and others will permanently take on positive or negative associations for me because of how they tend to appear in my readings.

Lastly, it's always wise to remember that the major arcana represents a cyclical journey, with all of us beginning the fool and all of us hoping to gain the world—materially and spiritually—before we start back over again. It's a nice life when we pull off such a journey once. It's a *great* one when we can reinvent ourselves over and over again; that's the way to growing ever older but never out of date.

# 0 THE FOOL

KEYWORDS:
*Fearlessness*
*Folly*
*Innocence*
*Potential*

You're going to hear the word "cycle" many times throughout this book, and here it comes again: as stated in the introduction to this section, the major arcana is a cycle, beginning with the Fool and ending with the World. It describes the journey of a person through life, striving toward material success and spiritual perfection. Not everyone makes it to the World before death, and some people complete many cycles over many lifetimes, becoming ever more wise and ever more *themselves* than they began. The Fool starts it all.

Childlike and optimistic, the Fool ambles curiously toward whatever piques his or her interest, much like the Pages you'll meet in the minor arcana later. The Fool's unburdened by anything weighty like experience or uncertainty, and the Fool will cheerfully amble into great adventure or off a cliff with precisely the same naiveté. Depending on where the card appears in the reading, sometimes it means that you're starting over again, and that you need to channel that youthful idealism, that fearless confidence that comes from having never been hurt. But it could also be a warning: Open your eyes before you walk into a fire pit; you know better!

# 1 THE MAGICIAN

KEYWORDS:
*Ability*
*Versatility*
*Control*
*Connections*

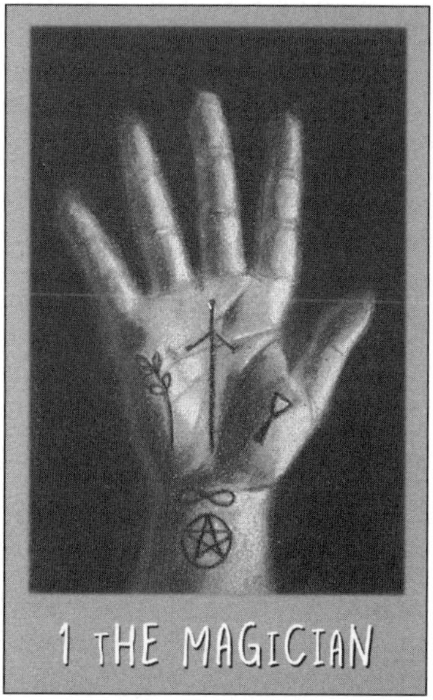


The Magician is no illusionist—he's the real deal. I have always loved the Magician card, as he is sort of an unsinkable ship; you can't keep someone down if they are always capable of building themselves back up again. The art on the card depicts a hand tattooed with all of the symbols of the tarot deck, and this is because the Magician has skill in all of the suits. The infinity symbol illustrates how his command over all of these suits comes from something outside him—if you believe in Something More; this is the Something More department.

Regardless of who or what you believe in, the Magician is an extraordinary master of all trades, and he is resilient because no matter what the world throws at him, no matter how much he loses, he will always have the most powerful tool at his command: himself. His command over all the suits actually gives him more power than the sum of the parts. Since he is familiar with all of the suits, he can find connections between them and use them to even greater effect.

When the Magician appears in your spread, it's a sign to let yourself be inspired by his powerful example. Remember that a truly powerful person is balanced and confident, equally at ease with logic, emotions, creativity, and hard work. The Magician tells you this is possible if you remember that your power is larger than your physical body.

# 2 THE HIGH PRIESTESS

KEYWORDS:
*Spirituality*
*Holiness*
*Dreaming*
*Unconscious*

In many ways, the High Priestess represents the art of tarot to me. She is a mystical force—unknowable, unfathomable, spiritual, and mysterious. Her secrets are not secrets because of deception but rather because they are mystical, arcane, and hidden until you are wise enough to discover them inside yourself as well. Like tarot itself, her power is interested in revealing the dark corners of your soul. Not dark as in negative. Dark as in *unseeable*. The High Priestess knows you cannot truly be yourself without searching for these hidden parts of yourself. The mirror on the card reflects you, but what you glimpse inside the glass is far more than your physical form. You are ever so much more than your body or even your mind.

When the High Priestess appears in your reading, it's a sign that you need to step away from external concerns and look inside. Embrace your unconscious. The High Priestess speaks in the wordless, strange language of dreams, a power that can only be harnessed by accepting that you won't always understand where your intuition is coming from.

# 3 THE EMPRESS

KEYWORDS:
*Mother Nature*
*Fruitfulness*
*Creation*
*Sensuous*

I chose a forest for the art on the Empress card because the Empress is often depicted as the Earth Mother. Indeed, she is the perfect mother archetype. She is loving, caring, and fruitful. It is not that everything she touches becomes fertile; it is that her fertility has created everything. The Empress is firmly fixed in this world, unlike the airy, moonlit High Priestess, and she adores everything good this world has to offer. Beauty, love, plenty, touch, sight—she is in love with all physical things.

She's also a deeply nurturing entity. You don't have to be afraid when you're in the presence of the Empress, because she is more than willing to keep you safe. She's powerful and nurturing, a lioness, and has an unforgiving set of teeth for anything that might come for her creations. That being said, she can be a little smothering. The Empress is not encouraging you to plunge after your ambitions. She's inviting you to stay in the comfortable bosom of the nest, to play and dine and frolic, to experience this moment with all of your senses.

When this card appears, it can mean that you need to go outside and literally enjoy Mother Nature, or it can merely mean that you need to stop and smell the roses. Take a moment to enjoy everything good in this world, all of its sensual pleasures, to love unconditionally, and to feel wholeheartedly.

# 4 THE EMPEROR

KEYWORDS:
*Kingship*
*Structure*
*Authority*
*Traditional*

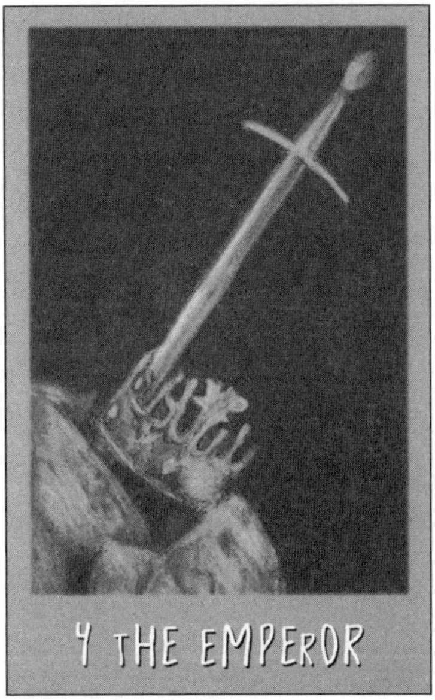


This is a very kingly card. All of the starry-eyed stereotypes that we apply to, say, King Arthur, are present in the Emperor. He's fair, just, stern, structured. He lives by the book… because he *wrote* the book. Just as the Empress has used her fruitful nature to create a world full of living things, the Emperor has created a world for himself too, and it's a world of rules and regulations, a world where everything goes right because there are dire consequences for when things go wrong.

The Emperor's kingdom is a safe and efficient one if you're willing to play by his rules, and most people are, because the rules are always there for a reason. Although the Emperor is not afraid to punish wrongdoers, he doesn't believe in being arbitrarily punitive. What would the point be? He leads by example, and that example only works if most everyone agrees that his version of right and wrong is true.

When the Emperor appears in your reading, he urges you to consider the role of regulations and tradition in your life. Depending on where the card appears in the reading, you might need to impose more structure, or you might find yourself chafing under rules you don't believe in. It's a good lesson, however, for a creative person to remember that even the freest of artists is still operating under rules . . . the difference is that they have made the rules for themselves. So remember that if you choose to slough off the authority of an Emperor, you must find the Emperor inside yourself.

# 5 THE HIEROPHANT

KEYWORDS:
*Teacher*
*Religion*
*Conformity*

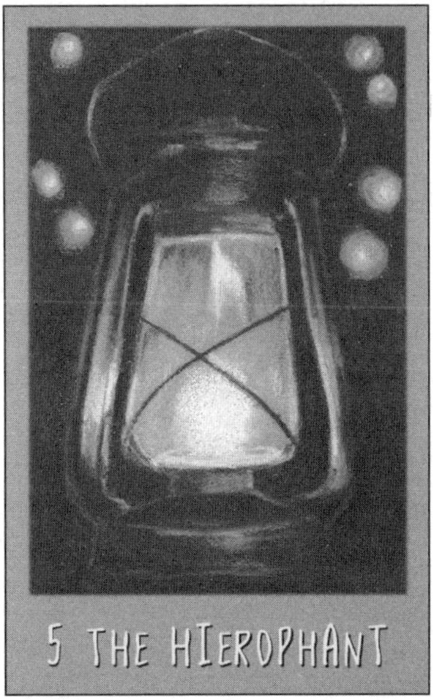


It seems strange that religion—structure, rules, tradition—is the external manifestation of something as nebulous as spirituality, but perhaps that's the only way we humans can cope with the possibility of something too big and too other to contain inside ourselves. The Hierophant is the external form of the High Priestess, and so, as expected, often represents religion or a person positioned as a religious authority. He is all about upholding the conventional establishment. Not just upholding, but growing it. The art on the card shows the spiritual glow of the soul safely contained in a lantern, safely contained in a way that makes it easier to pass from hand to hand.

This card can sometimes represent a belief system in its entirety, urging you to not make any dramatic or unconventional choices in a current matter, to stick with the tried and true. Or it can refer to a teacher or mentor appearing in your life, someone who believes in tradition and has a genuine talent for passing that passion on. In either case, know that the Hierophant stands for education and learning. Even if you cannot quite work out how the Hierophant figures in your life, it never hurts to dedicate yourself to the pursuit of wisdom.

# 6 THE LOVERS

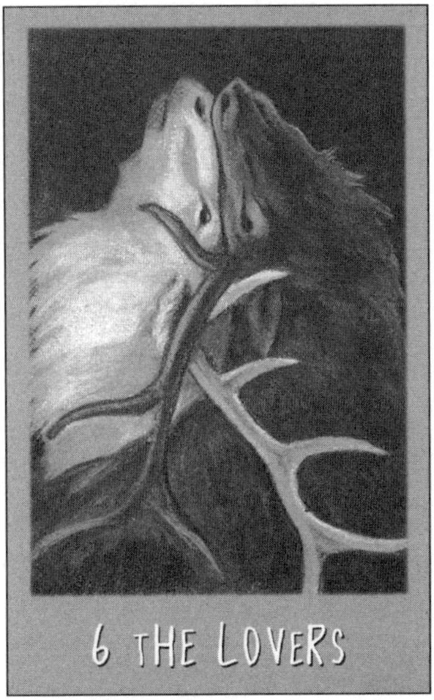


KEYWORDS:
*Love*
*Pairing*
*Duality*
*Values*

Nine times out of ten when this card appears in a reading, the person I'm reading for blushes and blusters. "I have no love life!" insists the embarrassed recipient. And often, they're right. This card *can* represent actual lovers, and when it does, the love pictured is epic—the pairing of two souls so complementary that it seems obvious that some greater power has designed them for each other. But it can also represent a duality inside you, and the complementary pairing it refers to is your inner self and your outer self. Just like in a great love affair, everything is perfect when both sides of you are working in harmony. And just like in a great love affair, the world crumbles when you war with yourself.

The card speaks to the power of wholeness and knowing yourself. It also represents a pair of lovers who are greater together than they are individually. This doesn't come from them being insubstantial or incomplete on their own, but rather from them being extraordinarily strong in two separate ways. When combined, they become profoundly powerful in a way that no one single person could be.

There's no need to blush when this card appears in your reading. All of us should have an eye on the Lovers, whether it refers to loving and knowing all ourselves, or whether it means finding our perfect other half.

# 7 THE CHARIOT

KEYWORDS:
*Balance*
*Self-Control*
*Duality*
*Id*

The duality that the Lovers card mutters about becomes a proper problem by the time the Chariot shows up in a reading. There are two sides to you, seemingly opposite, and you keep being thrown from one to the other. In many decks, this card depicts two beasts of different color pulling a chariot; when they agree on a direction, the chariot moves forward swiftly. When they disagree, the chariot grinds to a halt.

You've ground to a halt.

Oftentimes, the duality on this card refers to our emotions versus our intellect. The heart says one thing, the head says another, the chariot won't move. Other times, this card refers to our softer side and our more thrill-seeking side. This part of you urges safety, this other part of you shouts for risk. There's a reason why the dragons on this card are dark and light; they appear to be opposites.

When this card shows up, it's a sign that your self-control is being tested and generally is being found wanting. The chariot's not moving because you can't figure out how to get yourself in line. You can't figure out which *you* you want to be. The Chariot isn't really about choice, though. It's about balance. You aren't cutting one of the beasts free so that you can move on without it. The chariot will move with only one of them, but not as fast as if you found a way to make them both move in the same direction.

The Chariot tells you that there is a way to satisfy the warring parts of you. Find your self-control, embrace your dark and light sides, and enjoy the ride.

# 8 STRENGTH

KEYWORDS:
*Patience*
*Control*
*Self-Belief*

I've heard Strength interpreted in many different ways, many of them unsatisfyingly thin. I think the reason why it's a difficult card to interpret is because it can seem a little redundant. So much of the tarot deck is about internal strength that it feels like this card is meaningless when it appears. Be strong? Of course! What else would you want to be?

But I think this card begins to make more sense if you read it as fortitude in the long haul and if you replace the word *strength* with *patience.* When this card shows up, you *have* been being strong, but this card says that you're not done yet. Whatever burden you've been throwing yourself against is not going away any time soon, and you're going to have to dredge up all of your patience and self-belief to get past it. This card asks you to be resilient, a far more difficult task than mere strength.

The art shows a fist—the Magician's fist—held in solid belief. Remember everything you have learned about yourself before now and realize that you're going to learn a lot more before this is over. And don't just be strong. *Stay* strong.

# 9 THE HERMIT

KEYWORDS:
*Retreat*
*Wisdom*
*Spirituality*

I have a soft spot for the Hermit; I think every introvert does. The Hermit is someone who longs to retreat in order to better know their mind. Sometimes it is a straightforward pursuit of spiritual knowledge—a monk is the most straightforward interpretation of the Hermit. But often the Hermit is someone who doesn't even know what they need to know; they just know they can't discover it with all of the noise of humankind around them. Emotions often cloud the Hermit's judgment, and the only way to eliminate the messier ones is to retreat into solitude.

The Hermit card is all for this. If your instinct is telling you you just need some time away from a situation, or if your mind is begging you for some quiet, the Hermit tells you that you're not wrong. What's harder is when you *don't* feel that impulse, because the Hermit tells you that you need to remove yourself regardless. Sometimes you worry that the world will fall apart if you aren't there to tend to it. Sometimes you are entangled in a harmful relationship that you have been trying to fix; you know that to retreat is to end it. But in all cases, the Hermit says you need to tend to your soul first.

Give yourself a break, close your eyes, and listen for the wisdom inside yourself.

# 10 WHEEL OF FORTUNE

KEYWORDS:
*Destiny*
*Change*
*Farsightedness*

The Wheel of Fortune is a curious card, as it asks you to believe in the workings of something bigger than yourself. God, or fate, or even just the power of time with a capital T. Change is coming, it whispers, and you can't stop it, because it's been written … somewhere. Somewhere, something, someone has decided that things are going to get shaken up in your life. The Wheel of Fortune doesn't tell you if it will be good or bad, only that it will be different. The Wheel also reminds you that events and fortune come in cycles—so if things are good now, remember to save up this good feeling for when things inevitably go poorly. If life is hard now, remember that good times will come round once again, so keep your eyes up.

I chose to invoke the seasons for this card. Not only is the changing of the year cyclical, it, too, is something outside of our control. Instead of fearing the winter, we can remember the summer, and instead of wasting our summer, we can store our fruit for an easier winter.

# 11 JUSTICE

KEYWORDS:
*Absolutes*
*Cause and Effect*
*Morality*

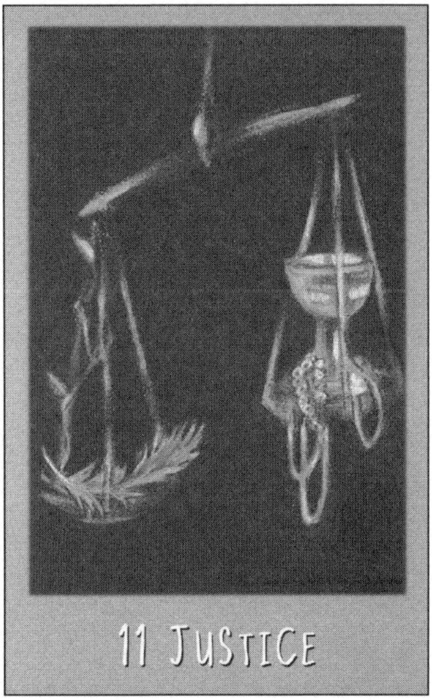


Justice is a bit like the morality version of the Wheel of Fortune. What goes up must come down; what goes around comes around; you reap what you sow; insert proverb here. When you see the Justice card, it reminds you that you may have fudged the rules a little and got away with it, or you may have persuaded others that your dubious choice was a correct one, but the universe believes in an absolute right or wrong, and you will get what you deserve based upon that.

This card is also a reminder that your reward or punishment is often unseen. A bad turn performed on someone else will haunt you years later, and likewise, an unnoticed kind event will create its own reward inside you. At the end of it, you will become the product of these actions: *you* are the Justice. There's an intense comfort to knowing that you have this control, especially if you feel your good intentions are being taken poorly.

# 12 THE HANGED MAN

KEYWORDS:
*Sacrifice*
*Wisdom*
*Self-Awareness*

I was taught that the Hanged Man of this card referred to Odin, who chose to hang himself upside down on the World Tree for nine days in order to receive wisdom. That potent image perfectly encapsulates the nuance of this card. The Hanged Man is all about sacrifice—not a martyr's sacrifice, but a scholar's sacrifice. He goes not only willingly, but pleasantly toward his hanging, certain that the time spent in agony will be worth it.

That's you!

When this card shows up in your reading, it's a sign that whatever answer you seek is not going to simply be handed to you. You need to level up in some way, and it's going to require a genuine effort on your part. It doesn't mean that it requires hard work or a huge sum of money (although let's be serious, it may require those too). It requires you to literally prostrate yourself on the altar of wisdom, holding yourself vulnerable, looking deep inside yourself for answers. You've got to let go and be willing to let knowledge and transformation take you.

And you've also got to be prepared to change. Because even though you might hang yourself on the tree only hoping for the correct answer to a single choice, you might find that by the time you're cut down, you see the world in an entirely different way. In fact, if you're lucky, you certainly will.

# 13 DEATH

KEYWORDS:
*Change*
*Transformation*
*Rebirth*

If I had a pony for every single book or movie that featured an ominous fortune-teller turning over the dreadful Death card, I would have a herd of glorious ponies and the world would be a better place.

The Death card has a powerful, fascinating meaning, and I'm sorry to report (although you might be glad to hear it, if you just turned it over) that it is not really a warning that your loved ones should buy more life insurance. It stands for transformation: complete, utter transformation, where you will be unrecognizable on the other side. What better to stand for this than the act of dying? We move from one life into another at death. We don't know exactly what the other side looks like, but we know it is nothing like this one. That uncertainty is what keeps us from willingly plunging into the transformation, even if we are in an untenable place in our life. We don't want to jump without being sure that there is a ledge on the other side of the dark chasm. Otherwise, we'll just stick to the reality we're sure of, thanks, even if it's truly dreadful.

When Death arrives in your reading, it's asking you to make that jump. Actually, that's not true. It's not asking. It's telling you it's already happening. You can be a willing partner, or you can be dragged, but you need to make yourself over one way or another; you've come to the useful end of life as you know it. Change can be terrifying, but it's exciting, too. Smile. It's gonna be cool.

# 14 TEMPERANCE

KEYWORDS:
*Moderation*
*Balance*
*Compromise*

I used to hate getting this card in a reading. I didn't know how to read it. Actually, that's not true. I knew exactly how to read it; I just didn't like it. I don't much care for moderation, or tempering my interests, or maintaining a healthy balance between work and play. I like zeroing in on a project and then going full throttle until either my body breaks down by the side of the road or I get to the end of the project.

Temperance suggests, gently, that I might reconsider this strategy. After the transformative experience of the Death card, theoretically we emerge as a somewhat more evolved being. We are beginning to learn to control ourselves, we're getting a better handle on what we want out of life, and now, well over halfway through the major arcana, is not the time to go dashing about after every short-term whim.

Instead, when Temperance appears in a reading, it's a sign for you to keep your eyes on the big picture. Instead of letting problems disturb you, let them wash over you. Unless they're going to affect your long-term goals, be slow to react. And if you're like me, obsessing over a project, remember all the lessons the major arcana has taught you so far: balance and self-control are what will win the race.

# 15 THE DEVIL

KEYWORDS:
*Addiction*
*Jealousy*
*Vices*

Well, this is ominous.

Just as the Death card did not truly mean death, the Devil card is not really about capital T, capital D The Devil. It is about lowercase t, lowercase d the devils that you have been carrying around with you. When I said that, you should have felt a little sigh escape you, because usually people are familiar with their personal devils. It can be addiction, self-loathing, jealousy, obsession. Tarot reminds us again and again that the worst villain lives inside us, and the Devil card is a warning that we are on a dangerous path. Often, when you pull the Devil card, you feel trapped, unable to improve your situation, and you can't figure out how to escape. What is keeping you here, bound like this? Why can't you just get over this problem?

The answer is *you.*

The imagery on the Devil card can be quite savage, evoking all of the fearsome Christian versions of the Devil: inversed pentagrams, horned beasts, perversion, and grotesquerie. Some version of that lurks inside all of us, which is why I chose a mask for my interpretation of the Devil. The scary monster that waits to unmake us is no other than ourselves. Check yourself, look inside, and choose to be a version of you that you're proud of. You know who that is. The Devil, for all its internal power, can't take that away from you. If you believe in yourself, you can easily pluck the mask free, but if you give in to the negative impulses, the mask instead becomes a part of you. Throw it away now, while you still can.

# 16 THE TOWER

KEYWORDS:
*Betrayal*
*Dissolution*
*Revelation*

In a dreadful way, seeing this card always excites me. Is it terrible to admit that? Most people find the Tower quite terrifying. The Tower is something that you have come to rely on, a truth you believe utterly, or a way of life that you have grown accustomed to. And in this card, it is entirely destroyed in a roaring, starving fire, leaving a blackened and unfamiliar territory on the other side of it. Sometimes it comes by surprise, this ravaging force that destroys something you thought was immutable. But usually it makes sense in retrospect. This is change that has been agitating for a long time, wisdom that has been battering at your mind, a truth that you've been refusing to admit. You've held it back, consciously or subconsciously, and now the fire explodes through your defenses, all the more savage for having been blocked up for so long.

The bad news is that it is going to be shocking, this revelation. There's a reason you've been resisting it. And it's going to be utterly devastating in the way that only a complete reversal or betrayal can be. Change is always stressful, and this is a huge change. The good news is you needed this. You didn't want it, but you definitely, certainly, absolutely needed it. Once you get over the wincing pain of having the rug snatched from under you (and the furniture taken, and maybe the house, too) and get your breath back, you'll find that you suddenly have a host of new possibilities open to you. You should've done this ages ago—it would've been a lot less violent, that's for sure—but it's over now. Dust the soot off your hands and start building something new.

# 17 THE STAR

KEYWORDS:
*Hope*
*Inspiration*
*Self-Esteem*
*Generosity*

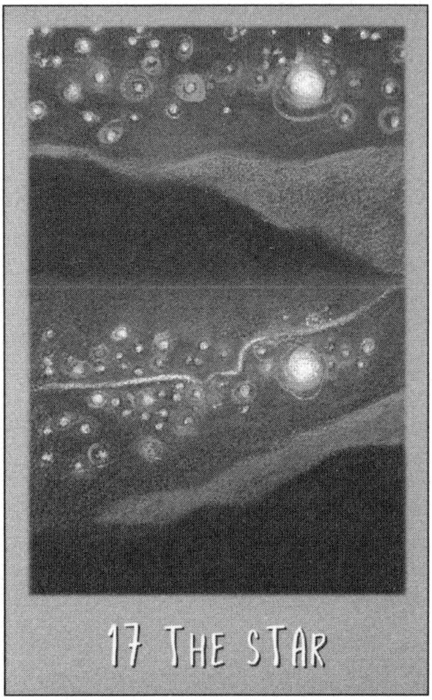


The meaning of the Star—hope, new possibilities, positivity—can seem somewhat frothy if you read it without considering the cards it follows in the major arcana. All that inspiration is nice, but it's not really . . . an *action* item. But if you think about how the Star follows the brutal Death, Devil, and Tower cards, the positivity represented in it is a pretty stunning accomplishment. Everything has changed for the person holding this card, and yet this complete turnaround hasn't broken them down. In fact, the opposite. The searing experience of complete personal transformation has left them a new creature, wide-eyed and wise, lighter for having shed their personal demons and false beliefs. The world is a hopeful place to the Star, and she is generous with her experience, freely telling the story of her transformation to those who are just beginning their own journeys.

When you get this card, it could be a sign to use your recent harrowing experiences to help others. It could also be an acknowledgment that the searing fire you just survived has left you feeling a little unsteady, and a nudge toward hope. You've survived, you've changed, and you are ready to move forward. You're wondering where you go from here? Anywhere. Anywhere at all.

## 18 THE MOON

KEYWORDS:
*Fear*
*Dreaming*
*Illusion*

Imagine you're walking in a landscape lit only by moonlight. Dark shapes surround you, and without any light, you can't be sure if that object closest to you is a boulder or a bear. You're pretty sure, though, that it's a bear. You hurry down the path—is there a path? There's not enough illumination for you to be certain that there's even a path. So you're just hurrying. On your way. Whichever way that might be. You're not sure if you're headed toward peril or comfort, or even if you're only going around in circles. The only comfort you have, really, is that the night can only go on so long, and eventually day will arrive with the sun and the clarity that brings. Until then, you'll have to make do with the moonlight and the unfeeling stars. This—all of this—is the Moon card.

Many people read the Moon as a negative card, and it's true that it is not a comfortable place to be, but I've never minded seeing it in my readings. I've always read it as a card of dreamy possibility. Sure, the scary part of this card is that anything is possible. But the wonderful, crazy part of this card means that *anything is possible.* A lot of good ideas can come out of this liminal space of tilting unease. Just like a dream, which might turn out to be either terrifying or wonderful, the ultimate tone is often decided by how you choose to view the world around you. Walk through the moonlit landscape expecting to find more boulders than bears, and you'll be surprised at how often daylight proves you right.

# 19 THE SUN

KEYWORDS:
*Solutions*
*Clear-Sightedness*
*Hope*
*Self-Awareness*

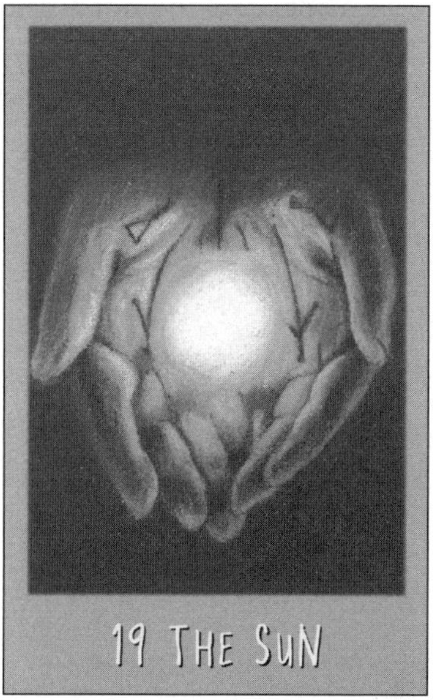


After the murky uncertainty of the Moon and the searing trauma of the Death, Devil, and Tower cards, finally the Sun has come out. With the Sun comes light and vitality and above all, *awareness.* You can finally see the truth with unbiased eyes. In the clear daylight, the world reveals itself to you, and finally, after the arduous journey to get here, you feel equal to the task of living in it.

The Sun is in many ways the opposite of the Moon, with all of the latter's veiled perils, but the Sun wouldn't feel like such a victory if you weren't so infinitely familiar with how it felt to stumble in the dark. The longer you've been wandering in uncertainty, the more you can appreciate this sudden, glorious surety.

When the Sun appears in your reading, don't doubt the hint of confidence you feel toying at the edge of your consciousness. It's not a fleeting mood. It's not unfounded. It's the beginning of a time of power and wisdom, of control and happiness. Hope and possibility have matured into joy and reality, so snatch the sun in your hand and use it to light your way.

# 20 JUDGMENT

KEYWORDS:
*Judgment*
*Meditation*
*Looking Back*

This is the second to last card in the cycle of the major arcana, and this card invites you to take a look at where you've been. Frequently mistaken for Justice and vice versa, it's simple to remember the meaning of this card if you think of it as Judgment Day, although it is not really an external reckoning. Instead, this is about you looking back over events in your life, using the objectivity given by time and experience to think about what really happened. Once you consider who you have been, whether you were right or wrong, how you have improved or not, you can decide who you want to be from now on using that wisdom.

When Judgment appears in your life, it's giving you a third opportunity to drastically change your direction. It's not the frightening transformation of the Death card, nor the fiery destruction of the Tower card. Instead, now that you've survived those changes, you're standing at a crossroads with an opportunity to become something new once more … this time with your eyes wide open.

You don't have to. You can stay the way you are now; this card isn't a warning. But if you want to have time to start the cycle back over again, to have another chance to begin again at the Fool and learn even more about the world and yourself, you're going to have to change.

This card doesn't tell you which is wrong or right. But I will! Slough that skin. Start over again.

# 21 THE WORLD

KEYWORDS:
*Completion*
*Accomplishment*
*Fulfillment*
*Belonging*

The World is the last card in the major arcana and represents the logical conclusion of a life productively lived. You're fulfilled in all the ways you could hope for: spiritually, romantically, creatively, materially. Life is good. There are bumps, of course—there are always bumps—but you've seen enough rough water to know how to sail through it without capsizing your boat. You feel connected to your family and friends, and you feel like you're doing the job you were meant to do, and you're good at it.

The World is yours, and when this card appears, it tells you that now is a time to enjoy everything you've achieved. This is a wonderful, productive time in your life, and you should feel it on every level. Mind, soul, heart.

Where do you go from here? There's nowhere to go but back to the beginning, to start the cycle back over again as the Fool with something brand-new. But for now, make the most of this joy. You've earned it.

# 6

# THE MINOR ARCANA

Originally, I tried to learn the meanings of the minor arcana from books rather like this one, and I found them nearly impossible to memorize. I dreaded their appearance in a reading; I had no idea how to proceed with them, and spent more time flipping through reference books than gaining any particular wisdom. Then several close friends did a number of readings for me, and watching them interact with the minor arcana completely changed the way I looked at them. Now I welcome them as practical, specific cards that often offer methods for putting the major arcana's wisdom into play in my life.

There are four suits in the minor arcana—the cups, coins, swords, and wands—and each of them stands for a different area of your life. They do have several things in common, however. Each of the suits is numbered one through ten and ends with four court cards: a Page, Knight, Queen, and King. Like the major arcana, the numbered cards represent a journey, with the one as the pure beginning and the ten as the fulfilled excess promised by the suit. The court cards generally represent an actual person—sometimes you, sometimes someone else in your life.

## THE CUPS

The cups suit is interested in the thing that we all can't avoid: people! This is the suit of relationships, both friendly and romantic, and all of the cards in it are interested in the way people come and go in your life and how you get along with them … or don't. It's a passionate suit interested in feelings and emotions. Interestingly enough, although fights and disagreements involve other people, you'll often find that the swords appear when you need to deal with that kind of conflict. In many ways, the swords are focused on keeping you from hurting other people. The cups have an eye on making yourself and other people happy. Complementary goals, but different methods: one positive, and one negative.

# ACE OF CUPS

KEYWORDS:
*Love*
*Beginnings*
*Friendship*
*Excitement*

The cups are interested in love and relationships, and the Ace of Cups, like the aces of all the suits, represents an opportunity or a beginning. When you see this, you're about to be faced with the possibility of a new relationship. Right now, it's just a tiny thing, like the baby bird on the card, but it has the possibility to be the kind of all-involving intimate friendship or love affair that we dream of. The kind of relationship that you hold on to for a lifetime.

Of course, like all of the aces, this is only a promise. You have to be open to such a relationship, which usually means being generous with your time and confident in yourself. The best relationships happen when you already like yourself; this easy step sidesteps a lot of the possible hurt or jealousy that could come later in the cups suit.

# TWO OF CUPS

KEYWORDS:
*Connection*
*Attraction*
*Intimacy*

This card logically follows the Ace of Cups—the promise of that close relationship has come to practical fruition, and you're now friends or lovers. I know this card traditionally makes this into a romantic union, but my relationships with my best friends are so close that I think this card could quite compellingly refer to that sort of intimate emotional knowledge.

The Two of Cups is closely related to the Lovers from the major arcana, but this card is still the first step in a relationship, much like the practical first moments of the intense relationship symbolized by the Lovers.

When you get into an all-consuming relationship like this, you need to remember who you are and what you believe in. Even though you feel like a stronger person in the company of the other person, you should maintain a sense of self outside of them. This card is hopeful for forever, but it is not a promise. Love yourself, too!

# THREE OF CUPS

KEYWORDS:
*Friendship*
*Celebration*
*Party*

Like the Three of Coins and the Three of Wands, the Three of Cups involves other people, but unlike those two, there's no work involved. It's the cups, the suit of relationships and friendship, so this is essentially a party card. It's a card about friendship, but not just two best friends—a group of people that you feel you can hang out with to enjoy yourself. How you define party or celebration or community is a very specific thing, however, so let this card reflect how you enjoy spending time with people.

Sometimes this card means that you haven't had enough opportunities to unwind with others, or it means that you don't feel as if you have enough people in your life that you *would* unwind with. In that case, take it as a goal, and keep your heart open. And in the case of all of the friendship cards, remember to be a friend to yourself first. Confidence and love attracts more confidence and love.

The ravens on this card are enjoying themselves; you can too.

# FOUR OF CUPS

KEYWORDS:
*Apathy*
*Waste*
*Taking for Granted*
*Self-Absorption*

Initially, nothing seems wrong with this card. It represents existing relationships that appear to be fine. They are not contentious. Everything is *fine.* But beneath the surface, things are not fine. This card is a warning that relationships are not being tended to. You're thinking more about your own needs than the other people in your life, and you're taking the great relationships of the first three cups cards for granted.

The good news is that this card is a warning. It's giving you plenty of heads-up so that you can reinforce those relationships again. Start asking yourself what other people need to feel comfortable. If it seems like a chore, ask yourself why. Is it because of something they did, or is it because other areas of your life are taking too much of your time for you to be a quality partner or friend? The best course of action is always to ask yourself how you'd like to be treated.

I chose reflected ravens to convey the apathy of this card. Gone is the joyful play of the Three of Cups; they're both thinking about themselves instead. That's no way to be a friend.

# FIVE OF CUPS

KEYWORDS:
*Loss*
*Solitude*
*Sadness*
*Grief*

All of the Fives symbolize adversity peculiar to their suit, so of course the Five of Cups is about the loss of a relationship. Sometimes this can be sudden and unexpected, such as a friend moving away or the death of a loved one. But more often this card hurts because you saw the parting of ways coming and couldn't or wouldn't stop it. Now you're stuck in an endless loop of wondering how you could have made it better or wishing that they would have seen the error of their ways.

The biggest message of this cup is not the loss, however. It's not a warning, like the Four of Cups, to change your ways. Instead, the Five of Cups appears when you're trapped in regret. All of your thoughts are preoccupied with what you've lost.

But thse art on the cup suggests the solution. Although the feathers symbolize the broken relationship, notice there's still another friend waiting nearby. Pull your eyes from the past and fix them on the future instead. Be grateful for what you have instead of grieving what you've lost and move on.

# SIX OF CUPS

KEYWORDS:
*Nostalgia*
*Childhood*
*Revisitation*

This is the nostalgia card. Its theme of looking back might seem very similar to the Five of Cups's obsession with what has passed, but I generally read the Six as a positive card. You're looking at the past, just like in the Five, but unlike in the Five, there's no pain.

Of course, excessive nostalgia can keep you from moving forward. The past tends to look rosier than it was, so it's not difficult to get caught in a stereotypical "when *I* was a kid" talk. Nostalgia can be incredibly stifling if all you do with it is compare it to the present and find the present constantly coming up short. But if you instead use your memories to be grateful for the life you've lived so far, and to remind you of the things that are important to you, they can be a powerful tool for helping you move forward. Sometimes you just can't figure out what you want out of the future until you compare your current state to what you wanted in the past.

The raven on this card regards six bubbles with child-like wonder, and often that is what the Six is asking from you. Revisit old memories, approach new relationships with the same innocent enthusiasm as you did before your heart was broken, and remember all of the wonderful things you've experienced so far. Keep a positive heart, and that list will only grow.

# SEVEN OF CUPS

KEYWORDS:
*Choices*
*Temptation*
*Options*
*Wishful Thinking*

The Seven of Cups shows a variety of choices, some of them immediately satisfying, some of them immediately deadly, and some of them spiritually enriching. When the Seven of Cups appears in a reading, it's a sign that you're facing a lot of choices … and many of them might not even be real choices. Instead, after the fanciful meditation of the Six of Cups, your thoughts are full of imagined possibilities, and it wouldn't be too hard to convince yourself that some of those daydreams might be actual choices here and now. Moreover, of the choices that *do* exist, many of them would do far more harm than good.

Now's not a time to choose at random, nor is it a time to choose lightly. This card has an implication of temptation, and because it's a cups card, it can often mean infidelity. It can also mean any other choice that will offer you immediate gratification but terrible consequences.

Step carefully. Among all the snakes and riches and prestige in the birds' beaks are also choices that will bring you spiritual fulfillment and satisfying relationships.

# EIGHT OF CUPS

KEYWORDS:
*Stagnation*
*Moving*
*Dissatisfaction*

I chose to use an image of reflected feathers on the Eight of Cups to call back to the reflected image on the Four of Cups. Both the Four and the Eight speak to stagnation and plateauing in your relationships. The difference is that the Four represents new relationships suffering because of neglect, and the Eight represents established relationships that are simply not satisfying. The situation in many ways has become untenable, and the longer you stew in it, the more nothing happens. Those floating feathers on the card aren't going anywhere without a wind of change.

When you see this card, it's an acknowledgment that your emotional situation is simply not working for you. Not only does it not satisfy you, it seems unfixable. When you imagine all the steps required to make it into a place you'd like to stay, you grow exhausted and continue to not move.

The only course of action is to take yourself out of the situation. You need to shed the things in your life that aren't working for you. It's time to realize that you have the power to be that wind of change, and whirl yourself away.

# NINE OF CUPS

KEYWORDS:
*Bliss*
*Fulfillment*
*Pleasure*

Happiness. I could leave that single word as the descriptor for this card, and anything you could imagine would be all right. The Nine of Cups is a joyful, wonderful card, representing all of your emotional dreams coming to fulfillment. Whatever you've been working towards in your relationships—be they friendly or familial or romantic—it's all here. You feel deeply content, and like things are about to get better. You're probably right.

The Nine and the Ten both represent happiness, but I generally read the Nine as being happiness that is inside you—optimism with where everything is going, where everything is at now, where you have been. You personally feel euphoric with the possibilities and actualities of your situation.

The art shows nine birds soaring in the clouds. The birds symbolize the strong relationships promised in the card and the clouds are … well, I just think it would be really great to be able to fly.

# TEN OF CUPS

KEYWORDS:
*Joy*
*Peace*
*Family*

I could copy and paste everything that I wrote for the Nine of Cups here, and add "but more, much more!" Both the Nine and the Ten represent deep happiness with the relationships in your life. But while the Nine represents internal happiness, the Ten looks outward at the reality and finds that indeed, it is as amazing as you suspected it might be in the Nine of Cups.

Don't squander this time! Enjoy it, because it can't last. Perfection is a moment, not a lifestyle. That's not to say that you will break up with your lover or lose a family member—there is no dire warning in this card—but part of what makes the Ten of Cups so idyllic is that everything is working together in a perfect balance. Eventually, someone will have a work crisis, or a move will have to happen, or a project will demand more time, and the bliss will be interrupted by real-world considerations. So frolic now, and store up great memories. They'll hold you through the next tough time and help you manifest the Ten of Cups again.

# PAGE OF CUPS

KEYWORDS:
*Emotion*
*Childlike*
*Innocence*

Like all of the pages, the Page of Cups is childlike, but the Page of Cups appears even more childlike than most because she is an emotional creature. She cries easily, laughs easily, loves easily. She approaches the world with childlike delight, without a touch of bitterness or judgment. She still believes in the power of dreams and goodness inherent in everyone.

She can sometimes frustrate the more practical members of society, because she's a diehard romantic. She's unwilling to compromise on perfection, and anything that falls short of her emotional ideal is likely to be quite upsetting to her. But you know who loves her? Kids. They can see themselves in her, and likewise, she can see herself in them. She can focus them in a way that she cannot focus herself.

When this card appears in your spread, it often means that you should try to channel her youthful dreaminess and emotional openness. Let others see how you're truly feeling.

# KNIGHT OF CUPS

KEYWORDS:
*Whimsy*
*Dreaming*
*Romantic*
*Fanciful*

Look at this dreamer. The Knight of Cups takes the emotions of the cups suit and wraps them around her like a fanciful cloak. Flirty, sensitive, idealistic—all of the strengths and weaknesses are in full force in the Knight of Cups. She has her head in the clouds, and unlike the Page, who is eager and willing to help, the Knight moves more slowly, preoccupied. This is not the person you want to ask to perform a practical task. Look at her! What is she so in love with? Love itself? Probably. Like the Page, the Knight can endlessly frustrate someone with a more pragmatic outlook.

When she appears in your spread, it could be an encouragement to allow yourself to make decisions with your heart instead of your head. But it could also be a warning that you are being too unrealistic. Whoa there, Romeo.

# QUEEN OF CUPS

KEYWORDS:
*Spirituality*
*Otherness*
*Mystery*

I very much enjoy this card—I'd like to be the Queen of Cups. She is spiritual, artistic, dreamy, and deeply in touch with her subconscious. She is supposed to be psychic, and even if she isn't, she appears to be because of her surprising insights into other people. She's a watcher, a mirror, a lover of the other side. She is very like the High Priestess of the major arcana, but unlike the High Priestess, the Queen of Cups is deeply interested in the affairs of other people. They come to her for advice and she uses her gentle insight to cunningly tease out secrets and wisdom, helping them to use their dreams to guide them, just as she uses her own dreams to guide her.

She can be easily exasperated by practical interests, however. It is not that she cannot apply herself to an everyday problem if it is handed to her; it is that she dreams spiritual wonders every night and can't quite see how you can imagine that paying the telephone bill on time ranks anywhere near as important in the relative scheme of things.

When the Queen of Cups appears in your reading, it's a sign to tap into your dreams and subconscious. I wouldn't be afraid of falling into the Queen of Cups's spiritually rich world of wonders and impossibilities, but then again, as I've admitted, I'm biased.

# KING OF CUPS

KEYWORDS:
*Calm*
*Counselor*
*Listener*
*Manipulation*

The King of Cups is a strange figure. Like all of the Kings, she is the master of her given suit, and like all of the Kings, she far more often dictates the use of her suit rather than dabbling in it herself. Only the King of Cups rules emotion, and so it is odd to see a powerful counselor who does not give in to her emotions as much as the rest of her volatile suit. She listens patiently to those who come to her in need of wisdom, and metes it out in calm, fair tones. She is generally good at this, and others appreciate that she can deliver emotional advice without getting emotional herself. She keeps her emotions under tight check, just as the King of Coins keeps her material wealth under wraps, and the King of Swords rarely uses her intellect to slice, and the King of Wands more often delegates artistry than creates herself. But the King of Cups's pent-up emotions can often escape in unpleasant, unexpected ways. She is well aware of how *others'* emotions work, and so she can be manipulative as she uses this knowledge to satisfy herself. She can sometimes take advantage of her position as an emotional confidante. She can also be somewhat superficial in her diplomacy, as she knows what everyone needs to hear.

When the King of Cups appears in a reading, try to channel her positive qualities—and there are many—of diplomacy and guidance. But also be mindful of subdued emotions. Better to be up front with your feelings, even if it means losing your crown. You can always earn it back later.

## The Coins

I'll confess that I'm not a huge fan of the coins suit. I don't find them unpleasant, just... not interesting. They represent the material world, the necessities in life, the nuts and bolts that keep your world running. I would rather not think about any of those things. Can't I just burn with creative fire all the time?

I'll spoil it for you: the answer is no. Although I happen to think a job in the creative field is the best job, only a small part of my life is involved with actual creating. It takes a lot of practical work to keep the creative life profitable, and a lot of times, you're just not going to get a chance to be creative if you don't take care of all of the other aspects of your life.

So even if you're like me and you'd prefer not to worry about practical considerations, you should learn to embrace this practical suit of jobs and money, creature comforts, and career planning.

I've chosen roses for the coins suit. If you've ever grown roses, you'll know they take a lot of work, and there's a lot that can go wrong with them. In a bad year, it seems like nothing can go *right* with them. But roses are rewarding as well; there's nothing like a rose garden in full bloom.

# ACE OF COINS

KEYWORDS:
*Potential*
*Prosperity*
*Beginnings*
*Opportunity*

The Ace of Coins represents opportunity. It is not a guarantee of concrete success, nor even a promise, but it's an open door. A possibility. Sometimes this card literally indicates a gift of money, or the successful securing of a grant or some other monetary windfall. Other times it is simply a shot at a new job. And sometimes it is the excitement of a career idea. Either way, the appearance of this card says *don't spend that money! Invest it!* Use whatever good fortune or energy this card represents to start something bigger.

The art on the card features a tiny rose seedling. Its best use is a long-term one. Plant it in the ground and find out what you need to do to take care of it. Don't feel discouraged that it's only a seedling; before this moment, you didn't even have that! And if you work hard, one day, you'll have roses.

# TWO OF COINS

KEYWORDS:
*Priorities*
*Balance*
*Change*

This card has a lot to do with that saying *time is money.* It is about balance and priorities; a lot of tarot art shows a man juggling on this card, because that's what it feels like. After the first blush of opportunity displayed on the Ace of Coins, things are starting to get a little complicated. You're feeling the pressure of balancing career with family, or perhaps having a hard time prioritizing multiple career concerns. The key here isn't so much about choice; you're not being asked to shed any of the things that you're balancing. The Two of Coins is about being flexible, willing to change and shift in order to accommodate the multiple demands put upon your time. Rather than stripping down to what you can handle right now, consider what can change to allow yourself to adequately tend all your concerns.

The art shows two rosebuds of equal size. A gardener could snip one bud off to allow a single bud to flourish more easily, or it could tend and feed the plant so that the bush can support both buds at once. The Two of Coins encourages you to do the latter.

# THREE OF COINS

KEYWORDS:
*Teamwork*
*Accomplishment*
*Satisfaction*

Well, this is great. The Three of Coins is a satisfying card, symbolizing the first real accomplishment in the coins suit, and perhaps the first time you realize that you're enjoying your job. The Three is fairly early in the suit, so there is a long way to go to completion and mastery, but the Three still feels pretty good. There's a strong connotation of teamwork, and the idea that your work companions are making this material goal satisfying to work on. The coins suit is not overly concerned with affairs of the heart, but this card suggests that you're happy at your work.

Depending on where the Three of Coins appears in a reading, it could mean either that you're enjoying a feeling of new accomplishment in your career, or it could also mean that you *long* to enjoy your career. It's a reminder that happiness at your job is possible, and is a worthy goal.

I chose partially open roses for the art to symbolize the relative newness of the endeavor; the glow over each is a reminder that this coins card, at least, also cares about your soul.

# FOUR OF COINS

KEYWORDS:
*Miser*
*Poverty*
*Possessiveness*
*Frugality*

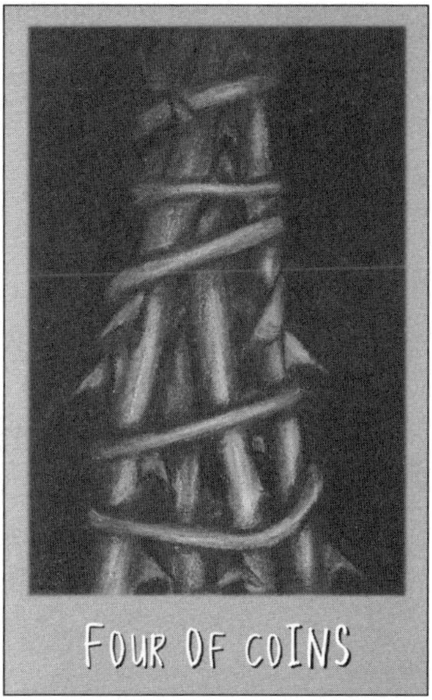


This card is nicknamed "the miser card," and the mixed feelings conjured up by the word *miser* pretty adequately sum up the possible interpretations of it. The core of the Four of Coins is that you're thinking about conserving money, rightly or wrongly. It might be because you have finally gained a little stability, and you're nervous about splashing out or making new investments—in this case, not so much being miserly as tight-fisted and frugal. It might be because even though you've gained a lot, you well remember what it was like to have nothing, and so you hold what you have close. It could be because you feel as if many people are asking you for money under any circumstance, and you're tired of your relationships being dominated by a dollar sign. If any of this feels like it rings true, consider whether you're being wise or miserly. Just because someone's asking doesn't mean you have to give, and just because someone needs doesn't mean that you must rush to satisfy. That said, sometimes you really are being called to help someone out financially, even if it's difficult for you.

This card can also mean the opposite: that you feel you are the beggar, with your hand always out. It's not comfortable to feel like you will never be able to stand on your own two legs.

This card can't tell you whether or not you should be more or less frugal. But when it appears, it's a sign that your relationship with money is strangling you like the vine pictured on the card. Even though money is only as good as what it can accomplish, you can't see the flowers of material wealth when you're holding the miser card. You'll find you only have a handful of thorns.

# FIVE OF COINS

KEYWORDS:
*Loss*
*Destitution*
*Poverty*

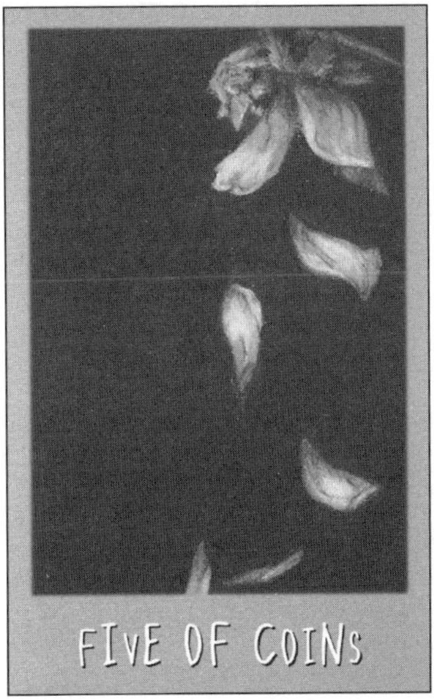


Let's talk about failure.

Like the other Fives, the Five of Coins is about turmoil and loss. The rose on the card sheds its petals; it'll soon be bare. The Five of Coins promises financial hardship, loss of a job, loss of stability. If not now, then soon. It might have been your fault; it might not have been. But with it comes a sense of failure and doom; you'll never be able to gain it back, you'll never get out of debt; you thought you were someone, but who are you now that everything is gone?

But the Five of Coins is only halfway through the coins suit: it's not the end of the world. There are five more cards to struggle through on your way to the top, and the only failure is in not getting back up again. Keep your chin up and remember that you are not your job, you are not your money, and you are not the car you drive (I love my cars; it was hard to type that last part.)

Often, too, the Five of Coins appears in a fearful position in a spread. It's not reality; instead, it's your deepest fear. Pay close attention to where it appears in the spread, because there's no point seeing chaos when it might just be reflecting your own terror.

# SIX OF COINS

KEYWORDS:
*Generosity*
*Contentedness*
*Charity*

I was sorely tempted to make this entry read simply: "Turn back to the entry for the Four of Coins and reverse everything it says." I'm not going to do that. But it's nearly true, nonetheless. The Four of Coins, "the miser card," is about being defined by an unhealthy relationship with money, either because you are being a miser or because you feel you're constantly having to ask for money from someone else. The Six, on the other hand, is about feeling good about where you are at with your finances. You feel stable enough to be able to think of lending a helping hand, or stable enough to *accept* a helping hand without it destroying your self-esteem. In either case, finances are no longer controlling you: you feel like you are controlling them.

It's worth noting that the coins are the suit of material goods and practical gain, so the gift on offer might not always be money. It could be hand-me-down furniture, donated time, or merely an act for someone else that requires a bit of sacrifice on your part. Sometimes the hardest thing to be generous with is our experience, so if there's someone in your life that might be heartened by hearing how you survived similar hardship, be mindful that your battle scars can be a gift as well.

The art is quite simply a gift of roses.

# SEVEN OF COINS

KEYWORDS:
*Assessment*
*Choice*
*Risk*
*Reward*

Decision time! The first six cards of the coins suit have watched you seize an opportunity, balance your priorities, learn to work with others, grapple with your material success, fall down, and then find your footing again. The Seven looks back at all of this and asks if it can be counted a success or a failure. Was it worth all of the work? Is this where you wanted to end up? Is there *more* than this?

As you look over this thing that you have built, it's time to ask yourself the hard questions. If you stay in this place, will you have what you need to continue to grow spiritually? If you choose to strive for higher ground, how much do you stand to risk?

The art shows a trellis with roses trained up it: hard work, and the blooms aren't open yet. The Seven of Coins can't make the decision for you, but it reminds you to take a good long look at your progress. Be honest with you how it makes you feel. Don't be ashamed if you are content; there is no shame to staying in this place and focusing on other aspects of your life, like relationships. And don't be ashamed if you find that you want to risk it all to move ahead. The Five of Coins showed you that it's possible to lose massively and still pick yourself back up again.

# EIGHT OF COINS

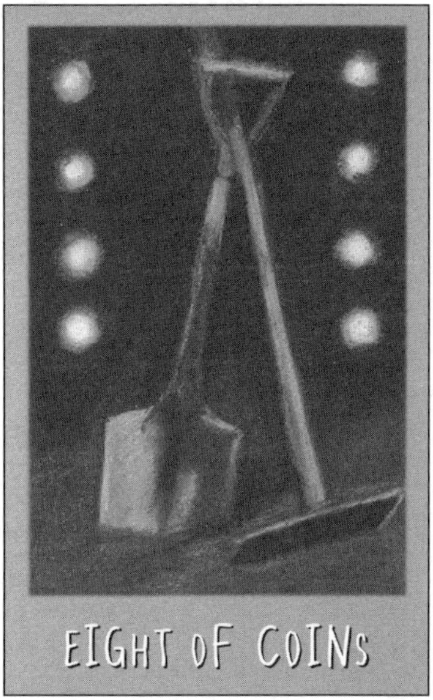


KEYWORDS:
*Workman*
*Stamina*
*Duty*

In art, in business, and in relationships, practice makes perfect. There's a fairly common belief in the world that artists somehow spring into the world with their craft fully formed, and another that the only thing an artist requires to be successful in an art career is skill. In reality, both of these things take incredible amounts of hard, unrewarding work to achieve. For every painting or novel or song that springs to life with effervescent beauty, there are hundreds of hours of repetitive practice that go unseen. Likewise, a career that looks like a miraculous overnight success story is generally supported by years of grinding but persistent laboring toward the top.

The Eight of Coins represents the person in the act of that diligence. You know what you're doing, you know where you would like to go, but there's simply no faster or easier way to get there than what you're doing. If you want the prize, you need these long hours and this relatively thankless sacrifice. If you're currently in this sort of situation when you see the Eight, take it as an indication to keep on laboring away—it's the only way through. And if you're trying to figure out how to take your career to the next level and aren't currently working your legs off, take this as a sign that you're not going to improve without some kind of sacrifice on your part.

I chose the shovel and hoe for this card. It's a card about work, and there's no point hiding the backbreaking truth of it. At least keep your eyes on those eight stars, though: whatever you're working on isn't just about the money. It's touching your soul in some way, or you wouldn't keep at it like you do.

# NINE OF COINS

KEYWORDS:
*Abundance*
*Satisfaction*
*Accomplishment*
*Success*

This is a lovely card to turn over when you've been working at something for a long time. The full bloom on the Nine of Coins—the first fully open rose pictured in the suit—indicates that your efforts have finally come to fruition. You've reached a place where you're not only stable, but you also have more than enough. Worries about material goods no longer niggle in the back of your mind when you sleep at night; you can now make career choices based upon what is artistically exciting or spiritually enriching for you, rather than what will put bread on the table.

That freedom is perhaps what makes this card better than the Ten, although the wealth pictured in the Ten is greater. The Nine of Coins is enough; it is plenty; it is not too much. It is just enough to allow you to be whoever you'd like to be. The coins are not a spiritual suit, but the abundance in this card means that you can now afford to turn your mind to non-career matters, which often makes it spiritual by default.

This card urges you to look around yourself and enjoy what you have. Do you need more? Have you been taking the time to bask in the other opportunities such success allows you? Don't squander it, but take the time to live. You've earned it.

# TEN OF COINS

KEYWORDS:
*Wealth*
*Generosity*
*Legacy*
*Excess*

This card is rich. It represents wealth beyond usefulness—everything you've wanted has come to be, and now you have stability, security, and all the freedom that comes from no longer having to worry about where your next paycheck will come from. The Nine of Coins also represents stability, but not like this. This is … *excessive.* That is the central conundrum of the Ten of Coins. Although it is a card of ultimate material satisfaction, it can leave your mouth a little dry.

You've clawed your way to the top of the mountain.

Now what?

This card urges you to think about the next generation, to consider using your excess material wealth for good that will outlive you. It's a good point; you need to do something for your spiritual health, so you might as well save the world, or at least your grandkids's college funds.

The art depicts a world stuffed with roses. Not just a single perfect bloom like the Nine of Wands. But ten perfect blooms, too many to see all at once, all competing for attention. Enjoy the ones that you like the best. But give the others to those who are just starting on their gardening journey. Be the windfall that the Ace of Coins predicts; start the cycle over again.

# PAGE OF COINS

KEYWORDS:
*Pragmatic*
*Responsible*
*Aspirations*

The Page of Coins is wide-eyed and optimistic like the other Pages, but unlike the other suits' Pages, the Page of Coins is responsible and pragmatic. The coins are concerned with material goods, and so is the Page. So even though she can be dreamy and hopeful as the others, she's perfectly capable and willing to funnel those nebulous feelings into an actual plan. She might not have the know-how, but she's good with details, and she's willing to learn. The coins suit isn't the most creative or revolutionary, but you can get a lot done within a conservative, traditional framework, especially if you have the Page's optimism.

When this card appears, it's a sign that you need to be like the Page and look for the opportunities that the Ace of Coins promises. The Page is the person to put those opportunities and windfalls to work.

The art is a tender shoot, striving out of the soil. It's a promise in a way that the Ace of Coins isn't. The Ace is about an opportunity, and opportunities can disappear. The Page is about being the sort of person who *uses* opportunities, and that is someone you can be forever.

# KNIGHT OF COINS

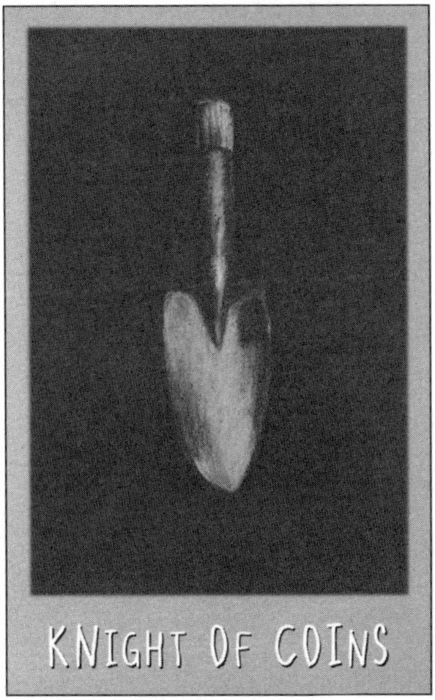


KEYWORDS:
*Dutiful*
*Methodical*
*Cautious*
*Hardworking*

The Knights of all the suits are generally swift and reckless; not the Knight of Coins. She is the physical embodiment of the Eight of Coins: dutiful and responsible, skilled and focused. She works steadily and without flinching in order to see her task through. Like all of the coins, she is traditional and conservative, favoring hard work over any of the fancy-schmancy innovation or feeling stuff.

There are some drawbacks to being the Knight of Coins, however. She can be stubborn, as she is certain her current path will take her to a project's completion, and she's not wrong. But that certainty can keep her from trying out anything new or taking a break. And she can be a little old-fashioned for the same reason.

But generally, the Knight of Coins is a good person to have on your side, and she's a good trait to have inside yourself. We all have times when we need to buckle down and just see a project through with dogged labor: the Knight of Coins is up to the task.

The art on the coin is the shovel from the Eight of Coins to remind you of the duty and workmanship that pervades both cards.

# QUEEN OF COINS

KEYWORDS:
*Nurturing*
*Maternal*
*Practical*
*Generous*

The Queen of Coins is the perfect mother: Mother to everyone! Mother to the world! She's not only giving and warm, she is *good* at it because the coins part of her personality means that she can sort of all of the practical details of being mother to everyone. She loves the material things in life, which makes sense, as she embodies the suit of creature comforts, and she loves making other people see just how comfortable and lovely the good things in life can be, too.

She can't do her work without security, though. It's hard for her to focus on the tactile pleasures of life if she has no place to call home. She thrives on stability, because it's hard to build a beautiful home when the foundation keeps moving. Don't begrudge her this stodginess; not everyone needs to be crawling with career aspirations or motivated by itchy feet.

When she appears in a reading, it might mean that you are the Queen of Coins or that you need to become more like her. It can also mean that you need a Queen of Coins in your life—and who doesn't?

The art is a flower crown, befitting a Queen who produces beauty, kindness, and comfort wherever she goes.

# KING OF COINS

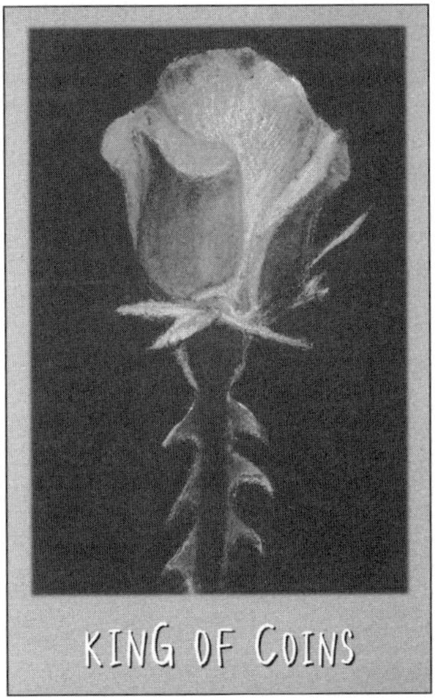


KEYWORDS:
*Business*
*Competent*
*Stability*
*Wealth*

The King of Coins has the best head for business that you could hope for, but you would never know it to hear it from her. She doesn't need to boast; she knows that the best proof of competence is in the actual result. And oh, does she have results. She is the personal embodiment of the Ten of Coins—absolute wealth and fulfillment—and she knows how to get results again and again and again. She knows the recipe of diligence and risk and firmness that results in practical perfection, and she sticks to it.

There's no one quite like her for pragmatic matters, and if you put an issue in her hands, rest assured that it will get done. The drawback to the King of Coins is that she embodies the conservatism and traditionalism of the suit. She knows how to get results, and she doesn't like to veer from that. Her own ideas work fine; she would rather not hear yours. She likes to manage other people, not listen to them. Not that she'll fight with you about it—she knows that levelheaded business is the way to go. She'll just nod and then do what she was going to do anyway, possibly sending you a memo later so you can note the discrepancies between her idea and yours.

There's one other drawback to the King, although if it's turned in your service, it might not seem like a drawback. The King is exceptionally slow to anger because most things just don't affect her quality of life. But when she does get angry, she will take you down with the same methodical diligence she applies to everything else in her life. The art shows the productive bloom that is the King of Coins's carefully crafted success; it also shows the thorns she would use to diligently disembowel you if you managed to anger her.

## The Swords

No one particularly likes being stabbed, not even metaphorically.

And yet that is what we find in the swords suit. The swords are the suit of conflict and argument, of logic and discussion. In the old days, arguments were settled by sword. In these days, we let our words do the work, and sometimes they can be even more painful. This suit generally appears when you need or are on the cutting edge of some hard steel. A reading that is dominated by swords generally indicates that you're undergoing a lot of conflict in your life, often untempered by emotion.

Artistically, I've picked hands to illustrate the swords. A nice compromise, I thought, between blades and words, and also appropriate to a suit where the conflict is often entirely contained within your own person.

# ACE OF SWORDS

KEYWORDS:
*Logic*
*Clarity*
*Power*

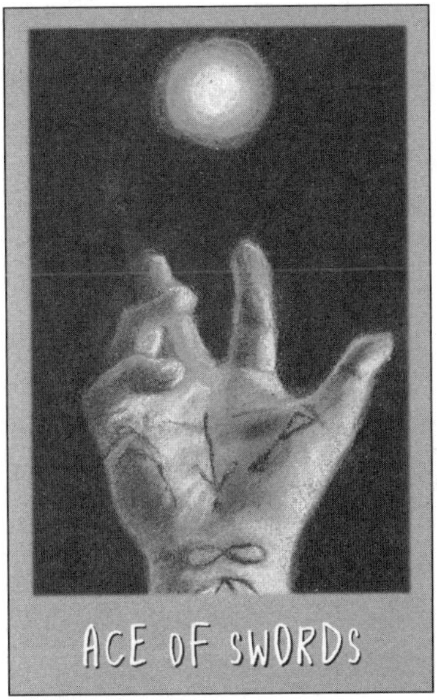


When you see the Ace of Swords, it means that you're about to cut through the gloom surrounding a confusing situation. The cool blade of logic can slice through all uncertainty down to the truth of the issue, neatly decapitating indecision. The Ace promises mental clarity, but sometimes at the expense of feelings.

It's impossible to talk about this suit without talking about the double edge of a sword. Logic is an effective tool, but it can also be the deadliest of weapons. Without the tempering softness of emotions, it can kill both attacker and defender in one fell blow.

When the Ace of Swords appears, it's showing you that you have an opportunity to cut through a cloud of conflicting feelings to the truth of a matter. In this case, it's probably a truth about *you,* which is why the hand on the card is reaching for a glowing star of inspiration. Spirituality and logic sometimes seem like opposites, but not in the case of this card. Use the Ace carefully to cut to the core of what you believe.

# TWO OF SWORDS

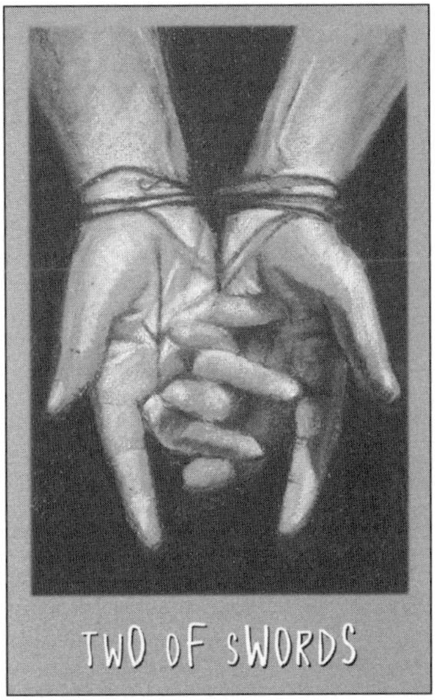


KEYWORDS:
*Duality*
*Decision-making*
*Choice*
*Stalemate*

The Two of Swords represents a war, only *you* are the battlefield and your mind has provided both of the armies. You're facing a choice, but both sides seem evenly matched, with nothing to recommend one over the other. The problem here, though, is that you don't really want to make a choice. It's easier to put it off—no one gets hurt that way. Especially not you.

Sometimes the Two of Swords represents a conflict where there are two parties, such as a fight in a relationship, but it's still a stalemate. There's no right or wrong, or there is, and both parties see it and refuse to voice it.

The hands are tied on this card, fingers braided. When it appears, it's telling you to be decisive. Choose to pull your fingers free of one another, and then you might find you have enough wherewithal to slip free of the rest of the tangle.

# THREE OF SWORDS

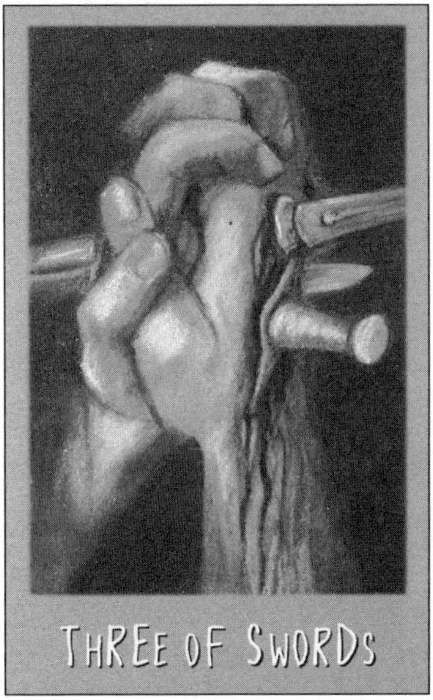


KEYWORDS:
*Heartbreak*
*Despair*
*Pain*

Congratulations! You've found the worst card in the deck. Well, perhaps not, but surely it is in the top five. Nicknamed "the heartbreak card," it does its best to earn the moniker. The pain symbolized in this card is intimate, personal, and devastating. Logic is often the weapon wielded here; it's the poison of choice in the swords suit, after all.

When you see this card, it's either a dire warning to step off your current path before things go to the worst sort of hell, or it's an acknowledgment of a situation you're already in. Needless to say, you'll easily be able to tell which.

Tarot skews positive, but it can be hard to see the positive in the Three of Swords. The most important thing to remember is that pain is transient; you will not be in pain forever. And hopefully whatever lesson you learn from this wound will help you in the future. Perhaps while you're being stabbed through and through it's not helpful to imagine how it will be interesting cocktail party conversation in ten years, but just in case, I'm throwing that out there. Troubled backstories are never a bad conversation opener.

# FOUR OF SWORDS

KEYWORDS:
*Rest*
*Recuperation*
*Exhaustion*

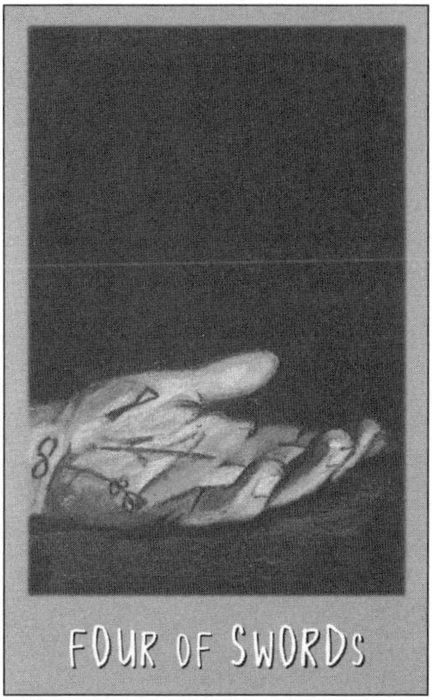


Taken in order of the cards of the swords suit, the rest urged by this card makes total sense. After the grueling agony of the Three of Swords, it's logical that you might want to curl up in the corner and pant in a sorry way for a while. If you pull this card in the middle of an otherwise active spread, however, you might be annoyed at its advice to be still and contemplative. The Four of Swords urges you to retreat or convalesce, to prepare yourself for the next battle—frustrating advice when you feel ready to go marching to war.

This card urges you to hesitate, however, and take a look at your emotional state. If you're coming here from the Three of Swords, you've been through some eel-infested waters, and you need to catch your breath. But if you feel prepared and surprised to see this card, the Four is asking you to double-check. Make sure that you've thought of everything before you plunge on. Are you really ready?

# FIVE OF SWORDS

KEYWORDS:
*Defeat*
*Dishonor*
*Pyrrhic Victory*

No one likes to lose. Certainly no one likes to go into a battle *knowing* they're going to lose. But that's what the Five of Swords is warning you of. All of the Fives indicate adversity, and in the fractious suit of the swords, it is uglier than most. The fight indicated by this card is an ugly one, with either you or the other party behaving dishonorably in some way—if not outright cheating, then bending the rules or otherwise ignoring ethics. It's also suggested that the fight is not really won by either party, and even if it is, it's a hollow victory. There was never going to be a clear-cut victory, and now there is no clear-cut defeat. The best one can hope for is a bitter compromise.

Or you could avoid the destruction this card warns of and choose *not* to fight. Be the better person, even if it means swallowing your pride or setting aside the conflict for another time. This isn't the time to push forward. It's never going to be satisfying, and it's going to hurt you as much as it hurts the other party.

The art on the card shows feathers falling through the fingers on the hand; even though you meant to keep a grip on the feathers, some of them were lost anyway.

# SIX OF SWORDS

KEYWORDS:
*Travel*
*Abandonment*
*Retreat*

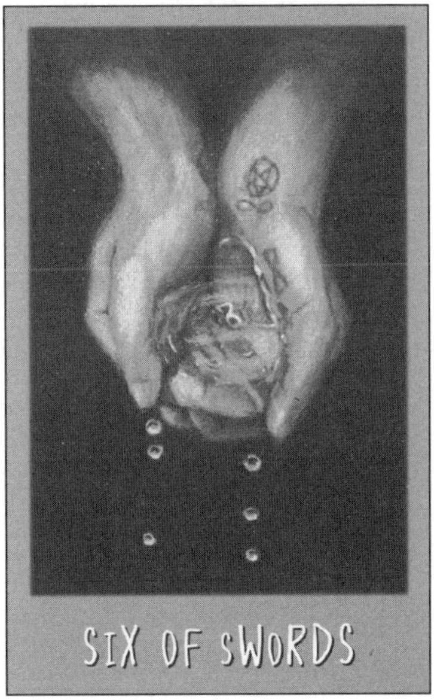


It's time to cut and run. When you've been in a very difficult situation for quite awhile, or when you've really gone all in for a fight, it's often tempting to consider any kind of retreat as a cowardly loss. But the Six of Swords urges you to take a look at the mess you're in and ask yourself if there's really anything productive to be accomplished here. Spoiler: there is not.

Because it is one of the swords suit, there's a healthy dose of logic inherent in this card. The art shows water pooled in your hands: lean forward and take a moment to reflect upon yourself. The Six is telling you to take a step back, but this is a moment to decide just how sizable that step needs to be. Sometimes it is a mental step, just stepping back from the argument. Sometimes, though, you need an actual physical change of scenery. The Six of Swords can't tell you how far to run. It can only tell you that you need a major shift in the situation for it to resolve, and that discretion is the better part of valor. Sometimes escaping can be the bravest thing you can do.

# SEVEN OF SWORDS

KEYWORDS:
*Deception*
*Strategy*
*Manipulation*
*Solitude*

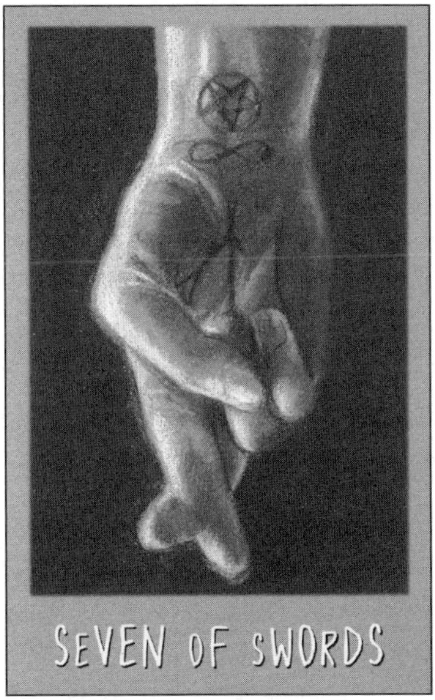


Although the swords are a logical suit, concerned with absolutes, they are not particularly fussed with ethics. Ethics, after all, are indeed absolutes, but they are an absolute of emotions. The absolutes of the swords often push aside principles to see the bottom line instead. They ask what will serve you best. Sometimes it means slicing other people along the way; sometimes it means doing things that you aren't proud of. Sometimes, living this way ends up with other people turning the tables and treating you this way, too.

This is exactly what the Seven of Swords promises. It is a card of cunning and deception. The kindest reading promises that this is a card of strategy—not out and out lying, just being cautious with the truth in order to get what you want. The worst reading admits that the word *strategy* often is just a pretty term for "manipulation". The person in this card often finds themselves in intentional solitude: too many partners will see through the web of half-truths. The Seven of Swords isn't always talking about you, however. You could also be the victim of someone's manipulation or lies, or perhaps be living with the suspicion that you're being played. Sometimes this card calls for a bit of gamesmanship, urging you to embrace your cunning.

Personally, I nearly always think it's better to uncross my fingers and tell the truth. It can be tempting to play the game, but in the end, blades hidden in the murk—even your own—are more likely to cut you than ones clearly presented in the light of day.

# EIGHT OF SWORDS

KEYWORDS:
*Self-Doubt*
*Confusion*
*Imprisonment*
*Control*

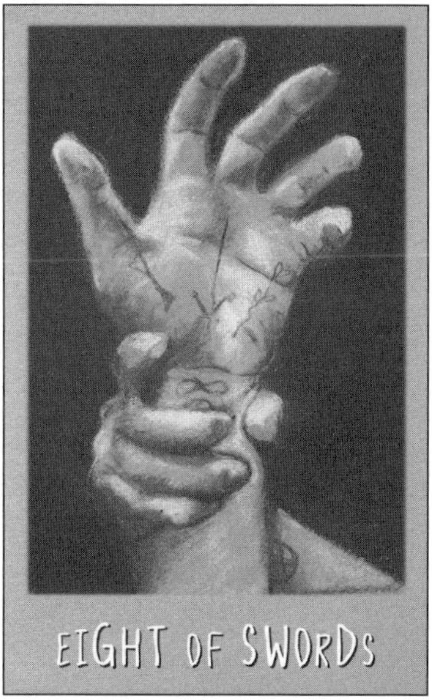


When you pull the Eight of Swords, you've finally met your worst enemy, the enemy that the tarot deck constantly talks about but rarely points fingers directly at. The Devil card points firmly at this enemy, though, and so does this card.

That enemy is you.

Nearly every artistic interpretation of this card involves some kind of binding; the original Rider-Waite art features a woman who is blindfolded, loosely tied, and surrounded by swords. Her binding is so loose that at any point, she could choose to slip her hands out, pull down her blindfold, and tidily step out of her self-imposed prison of swords. Likewise, on my card, the right hand grips the left. There is no other attacker: *you* are the assailant *and* the victim.

When this card appears, it's good news and bad news. You have all the tools you need to escape your current painful situation. You don't need to go looking, you don't need to strive for more weaponry. It's right there, and it could be over today. But the bad news is that you don't want to, and you are, after all, your most powerful enemy. Something is keeping you in place—self-doubt, confusion about what you really want, or perhaps certainty that what you really want goes against your principles in some way. A battle rages inside you, and so you remain utterly motionless.

The Eight of Swords urges you to realize that you are the problem here—not any of the excuses you've made—and to use that knowledge to find a solution. Now's the time to realize that you have control, whether or not you want it. Take the wheel and drive out of this place.

# NINE OF SWORDS

KEYWORDS:
Depression
Introversion
Fear

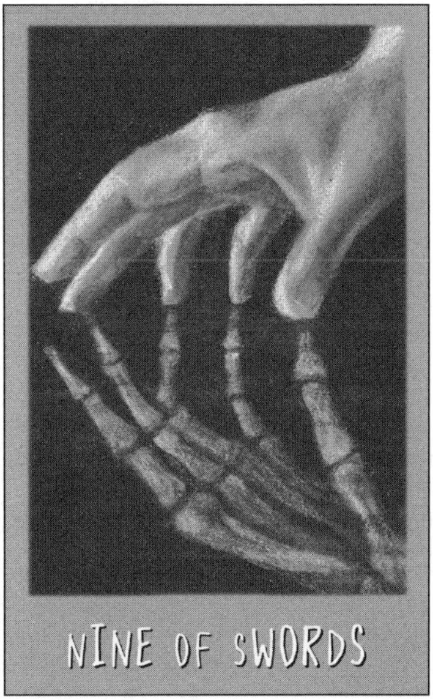


This card is perhaps the most fearful in the deck, which is impressive, because when it appears, there may, in fact, be absolutely nothing to be afraid of. Of course, there might be everything to be afraid of, too, but this card isn't particularly concerned with that. The Nine of Swords looks at the weather conditions inside you, not outside your window, and the report is one hundred percent rain with a chance of hail or the end of the world.

This is the depression card. Whether it is earned or not, you cannot stop yourself of thinking of the worst. Sometimes it's something that's already happened, something you can't forget—maybe the heartbreak of the Three of Swords—or maybe it's something that you fear will happen—maybe the absolute ending of the Ten of Swords. Either way, you live in a toxic black mire of fear or guilt.

It's not wrong to feel this way, but it's impossible to *live* this way. Nothing gets done when you're in the Nine of Swords. Everything turns inward, and eventually your introspection paralyzes you entirely. Unlike the Four of Swords, which encourages inaction, the Nine of Swords isn't condoning this paralysis. This isn't useful introspection; you're not meditating or learning anything about yourself. Get up, dust yourself off, and start making active solutions.

# TEN OF SWORDS

KEYWORDS:
*Suffering*
*Illness*
*Tragedy*
*Endings*

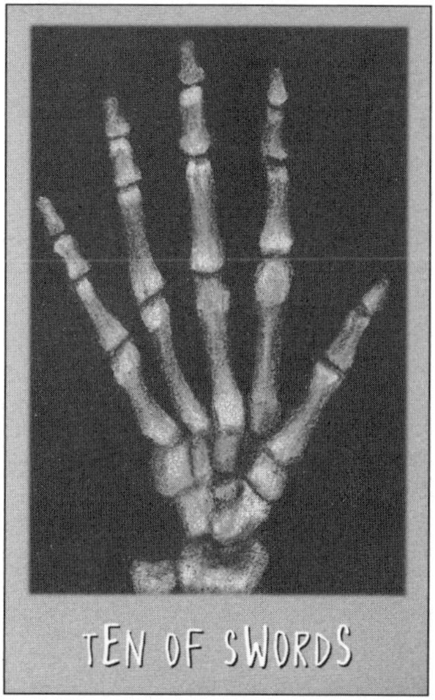


There's no point in sugar-coating this card: it's pretty terrible. On the traditional Rider-Waite deck, the art features a man stabbed with ten swords, which seems excessive. My art has settled for bare bones, literally, but the meaning is the same: an ending, and a bad one. This card warns of an agonizing and brutal conclusion, and the worst part is that it quite probably was your own fault. Back at the beginning of the suit, the Ace promised the double-sided power of the swords suit, and along every step of the way, the swords cards have whispered of the dangers of power and logic when freed from empathy and mercy. Often this card is a result of you ignoring those warnings and now you reap the black harvest that you sowed. You might not agree—martyrdom is often associated with this card—but it doesn't really matter if you think this is an unjust punishment. Stabbed is stabbed. It's over.

There's a bright side, though, and that's that this is the worst it will get. There's no eleven of swords to kill you even deader. When you've hit rock bottom, there's nowhere to go but up.

# PAGE OF SWORDS

KEYWORDS:
*Truth*
*Learning*
*Seeking*
*Clarity*

The Page of Swords wants to *know.* She wants to know the truth of matters, she wants to know how things work, she wants to sort through the gray until she finds just how much black and white have been used to make it. Using the energy of the Ace, she is full of clear-headed ideas and clinical curiosity. Like all of the Aces, she is childlike and optimistic, and when she appears in a reading, it means that you should channel the unbiased interest of a child.

She's also tireless in her pursuit of the truth, and the appearance of this card might be urging you to do the same. Clear away all the bad feeling, doubt, and emotional biases you might have gained from negative experiences in the world, and use the energy of the swords to cheerfully cut to the heart of the matter.

# KNIGHT OF SWORDS

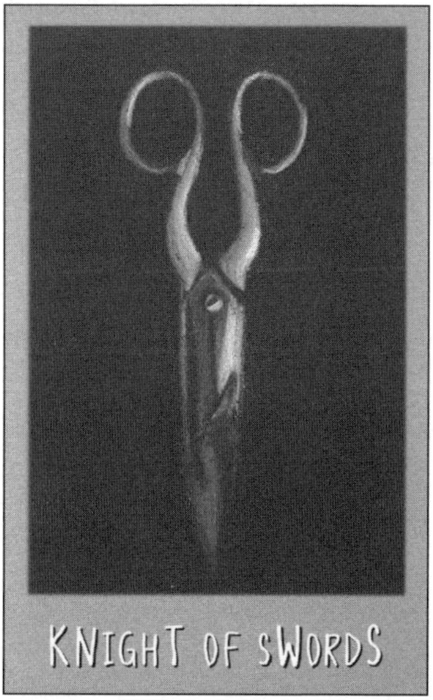


KEYWORDS:
*Confrontation*
*Hostility*
*Directness*
*Logic*

The villagers hide under their beds when the Knight of Swords arrives. Like all of the Knights, she acts the most swiftly of her suit's court cards, and in her case, she moves swiftly with the ruthless logic of the swords. Heads roll; she doesn't care. Right is on her side—she has no fear, and she is unburdened by the fear that she will destroy other people's confidence. She has seen the solution and she will see it through, even if there's blood drawn.

Of course, with the swords, the blood in this case is usually emotional blood. The Knight of Swords has her feelings well in check, and so the blood is not hers. This can be good and bad; if you've been waffling over a situation, the Knight can be a push to plunge in and slice ferociously to the truth of the matter. Often everyone will see things more clearly after they get done wincing, and the situation can move ahead. But sometimes, when the Knight appears, it's a warning that you're being a little too focused on the problem and not focused enough on other people's feelings … especially your own. Because that's the true strength and fault of the Knight of Swords. The blood-tipped scissors on the card come from plunging words into someone else's heart, but the person who wielded them was only able to do so by silencing that tempering voice inside themselves.

All of us need to be the Knight of Swords sometimes. None of us needs to be the Knight of Swords all the time.

# QUEEN OF SWORDS

KEYWORDS:
*Clarity*
*Honesty*
*Critical*
*Insightful*

The Queen of Swords sees the harsh, cold truth of everything, and then she tells people about it. She isn't in touch with her emotions—not because they are blocked, but because she doesn't see the value in them—and so there's nothing to temper the truth. It isn't that she is wrong. It's that she can't stop herself from revealing the truth, no matter how hurtful it is. Sometimes this is useful, because it can be hard to be objective about a bad situation when you're in the middle of it, and it can be nice to have a clever and impartial judge to help you make a choice that stymies you.

But often the Queen of Swords finds herself alone. Her wise sword has too much blood smeared on it to provide comfort. Truth, the whole truth, is often too much, especially if the other party feels that you're not applying the same level of harsh discernment to yourself. And the

Queen can seem cruel, too, because sometimes she *is:* when she's feeling low, she can't resist getting in a jab here or there.

When this card appears, the cutting blade emerging from the pool of truth, it sometimes means that you need to be the Queen, powerful and in control of your emotions, wise and impartial. And sometimes it means that you feel that you are being unfairly seen as the Queen—you might be an undemonstrative person, or you might be frustrated by friends or family who seem unwilling to change obvious problems in their lives. And sometimes you really are the Queen of Swords with all her thin truth, facing an alien field of other people's emotions. If that's the case, you don't have to learn to give comfort. You only have to learn to sometimes hold your tongue.

# KING OF SWORDS

KEYWORDS:
*Just*
*Fairness*
*Intellect*
*Truth*

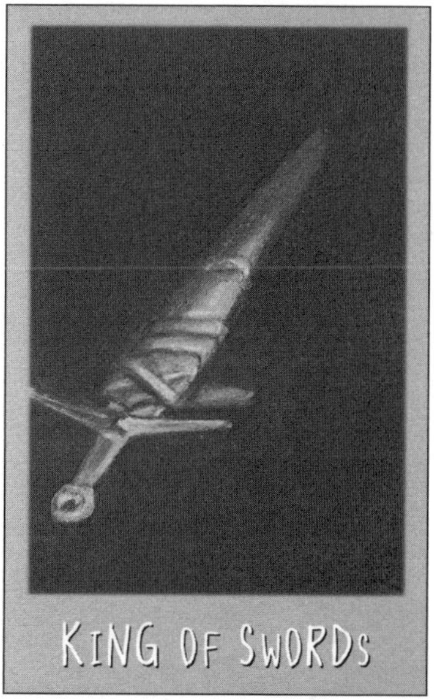


Unlike the bitter truth of the Queen, the King of Swords's opinion is valued, because she doesn't offer it unless required. Rather than meting out cruel truths at every turn, the King has learned to be judicious about sharing the things that she knows. And oh, the things she knows! The King is the logical product of a lifetime of valuing the truth, of valuing facts, of valuing the secret details that often escape others.

Unlike the other swords court cards, which don't have much use for emotions or morality, the King is quite interested in both of these things. It is not that she *has* them. It is that she sees the big picture, and she has observed that many other people, in fact, have emotions and morality, and one simply cannot make good decisions without taking those into account. As such, she is often consulted for wisdom, unlike the Queen, who is avoided for the same truth.

The King also does not take herself into account when she is making decisions, and so one can be sure her opinion is unbiased.

The sword on the card is sheathed; the King of Swords can be ruthlessly and sociopathically fearsome when crossed, but that almost never happens. Why would someone cross her? She stands for truth and the law. The sword remains covered, and the world is grateful.

## The Wands

I confess I'm badly biased—the wands are my favorite suit. They're the suit of creativity, so it's always comforting to see a healthy representation of them in a spread. Like all of the other suits, they represent a life cycle of sorts, with the fiery Ace birthing an idea and the Ten standing for the weighty conclusion of it. And like the other suits, the absence of them can mean as much as their presence. If I ask myself which of two projects I should tackle and find myself looking at a spread bereft of wands, it means I need to consider factors outside of the actual *making* of the project.

# ACE OF WANDS

KEYWORDS:
*Creativity*
*Energy*
*Passion*
*Enthusiasm*

This card symbolizes raw creativity. Inspiration. Beginning. Opportunity.

As an artist of many sorts, I love pulling the Ace of Wands. It's giving me permission to fall in love with a brand-new project, to start something new, to hurl kindling onto a tiny spark of an idea. The longer I practice my art, the more patient I tend to be with new projects—I let them linger inside my mind until they're ready for me to make them a physical thing. This hibernation period makes for nuanced and specific art, but it also makes it easy for a project to never *feel* ready.

The Ace of Wands means that sometimes you're not going to ever *feel* ready. Act now. Just jump! If you're a perfectionist, it can be hard to accept that a new idea doesn't arrive fully formed. It's imperfect, underdeveloped, sometimes ugly, and other times hard to explain to others. If it was anything more, it wouldn't be the Ace. The Ace isn't for anyone else. It's for you.

Of course, there can be drawbacks. Like most new love, the Ace of Wands burns hot, fast, and pure—it can be a little too single-minded in its absorption over a new project. Often, other things will be obscured by the light of its furious flashpoint.

I tend to say let the wildfire take you; this is an opportunity you're not going to want to pass up. Even if it goes terribly wrong, it'll be memorable. When you see this card, let loose and fan the flames. A fiery journey is underway.

# TWO OF WANDS

KEYWORDS:
*Planning*
*Goals*
*Looking Forward*

Ideas are fantastic, but everyone has them. A rather smaller group actually acts productively on them. That's where the Two of Wands comes in. After the creative rush of the Ace, it's time to look ahead. Where are you going with this? What's your long-term goal? It's still a long way off, but what's the best possible scenario you can imagine for this youthful creative project in your hands?

I chose a raven snatching a wand from the creative fire for the Two because that's how it feels to me: artistic chaos roars ferociously, powerful but lacking direction. In the Two of Wands, my logical self begins to impose structure and direction on that idea. The raven snatches the burning branch out of the bonfire. It's a smaller flame, not as blinding as the Ace, but it's also controllable.

When you pull the Two of Wands, it's time to make some goals for yourself. They should be personal goals, milestones that are entirely within your power to achieve. It's not time to release your creative force on the world yet, but it's time to start thinking about it.

# THREE OF WANDS

KEYWORDS:
*Growth*
*Partnership*
*Planning*

Often, one of the most alarming steps in a creative project is the first time you have to show it to someone else. Until this point, you may have dreamed of sharing your plan with others, but you weren't really certain of how it would be received. Possibly, it will only make sense to you. Possibly, it's just not good enough to share with others yet, even in a preliminary way. Fear can keep you alone, and can also effectively extinguish the creative force of the Ace and Two of Wands. A lack of imagination can also keep you from moving forward—an inability to see a big picture where others are involved, either in the process of the project, or as the audience.

But the Three of Wands says that now is the time to think about others. Sometimes it means to collaborate, or to seek advice, or merely to turn your page to the class so that you can judge their reactions.

I chose a raven—your intellect—guarding established embers for the Three of Wands because the Three of Wands refers to something that's already been undertaken. It is not a ferocious flame that needs to be tamed; it's a campfire that requires your attention in order to persist. It's also a fire that would look good with friends sitting around it. Give it a shot. Shoot the breeze by the embers and keep thinking big.

# FOUR OF WANDS

KEYWORDS:
*Stability*
*Resting*
*Happiness*
*First Completion*

Like all of the Fours, the Four of Wands represents stability of some kind. In many decks, the art on this card features a wedding, and that's a pretty solid way to read this card. A wedding is both an ending and a beginning: end of a courtship, beginning of a life together. It's a joyful resting spot, but it's not a place to stay. The Four of Wands signals some kind of completion: a moment to pause and admire what you've accomplished, often with friends. You've felt the creative fire in the Ace, tamed it in the Two, established it in the Three, and now you find yourself in the agreeable liminal space of the Four.

I've chosen four candles for the art; firstly because they are a stable form of the fire of the first three cards, and secondly because I tend to read this card with slightly more dissatisfaction than most. I'm a restless soul, always jonesing for the *next thing*, and any sort of pause tends to make me itchy. It's good to learn to appreciate the pleasant celebration of this card, and there's nothing wrong with longing for it after the work of the first three wands in the suit, but four diminutive candles are far from endgame for the fiery potential inside you.

Enjoy the moment, but keep your eyes up: there's farther to go.

# FIVE OF WANDS

KEYWORDS:
*Chaos*
*Priorities*
*Competition*

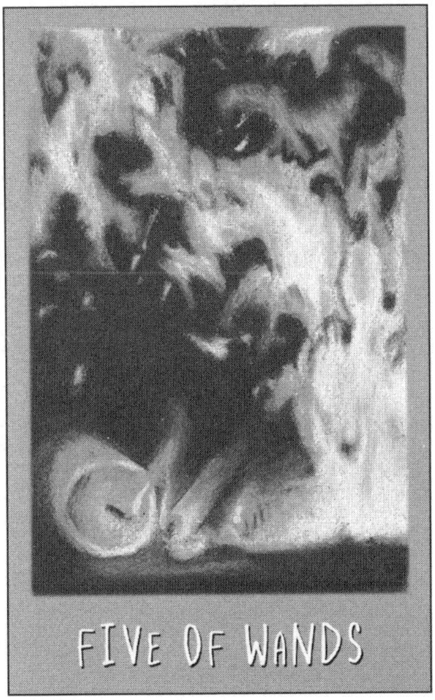


Well, things have gone pear-shaped.

Things haven't been ... *easy* in the first four cards of the wands cycle, but at least most of what you've had to fight is *yourself.* The Five of Wands is the first time major conflict appears in the wands suit, and it comes from the shift from the internal process of the first four cards to the often external interests of the latter cards. You and your ideas have plunged into the world now, and it turns out there are other people in this world. And it also turns out those other people don't always think the same way you do. For the first time, you have to defend what you do. Or, more often, since this card is sandwiched between internal and external cards, *why* you do what you do.

The assault you feel in this card comes from multiple directions, but it's not a single army. It's a host of dissonant voices rising against you, questioning your ethics, so you cannot use the same defense against each of them. It's often easy to feel as if your personal projects and concerns can't move forward because you're spending all of your time defending yourself.

The art for this card is as fiery as the Ace of Wands. Intentionally so, because the chaos of the Ace is definitely back, just without the delight of new discovery. You're going to have to once again snatch your project from the chaotic firmament. But this time, unlike with the Ace, you have experience. You've got this. You know how to do this when there are no voices questioning you; now's the time to relearn how to focus while the world shouts in your face.

# SIX OF WANDS

KEYWORDS:
*Victory*
*Achievement*
*Pride*

Pop the champagne! This card is a good excuse to open the bubbly, if you are a fan of champagne. I'm not, but I'd do the Maggie equivalent—treat myself to a new set of racing tires or something. Because the Six of Wands has a quite singular meaning: victory. After the chaotic distraction of the Five, you've emerged triumphant and you're being recognized for your achievement. It might be a massive victory: winning a race, getting published, being recognized as the cake-eating champion of North America. Or it might be as simple as your boss nodding firmly in appreciation of your work. The most important aspect is that you have put yourself out in the world, and the world gave you a thumbs-up.

It feels great.

Don't let it go to your head—you deserve a boost of confidence when this card shows up, but remember, there's always more to learn. And pay attention to where the Six appears in a spread. Sometimes it is not promising or acknowledging a victory. Sometimes it is telling you that you're making external validation a goal, or that you need some sort of feeling of accomplishment to move on.

The art is quite simply victor's laurels. Enjoy the champagne or racing tires.

# SEVEN OF WANDS

KEYWORDS:
*Strategy*
*Priorities*
*Defense*

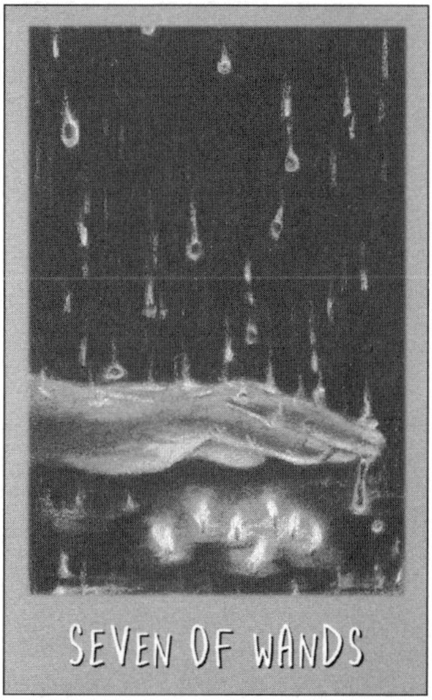


It's time to defend yourself. You have the high ground, so at least you can hold that knowledge close as the enemy comes at you. When the Seven of Wands appears, it usually means that you find yourself being attacked, often on a personal level. Unlike the Five of Wands, where the world is coming at you from multiple directions without coordination, the threat in the Seven of Wands is more united. You're outnumbered, with only your wits, experience, and principles to bolster you. You'll need to be strategic to protect yourself, your ideas, and your projects. They might be asking you to explain yourself, to defend your choices, wanting to toss you from your seat at the feast. Rally all your wits and confidence to keep yourself on course; sometimes just being good at what you do won't be enough. There may be shouting involved.

I chose an image of a hand sheltering the creative flames from the pelting rain that would dowse them, because that is what you need to protect in all of this: the fire inside that makes you uniquely *you.* Stay the course, be as clever as you can, and don't compromise your principles.

# EIGHT OF WANDS

KEYWORDS:
*Quick Action*
*Force*
*Movement*

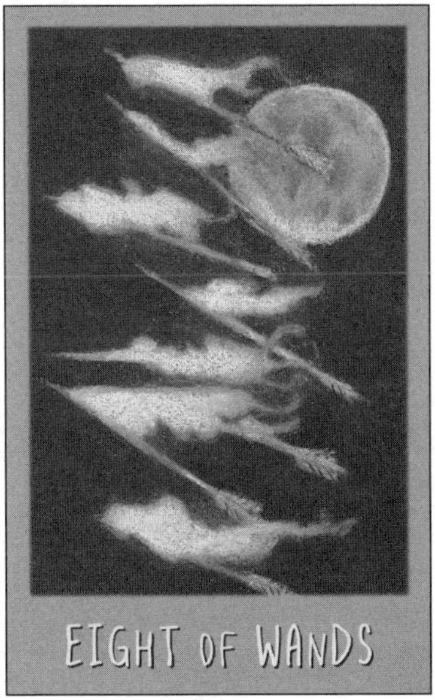


Finally. *Finally.* Everything has fallen into place when the Eight of Wands appears. You have a goal in mind. Experience surges through you; you know you have the skills to accomplish it. There might be a few obstacles, but even they are easily surmountable: you already know how you're going to tackle them. So now's the time to move. Don't hesitate, because this wide-open opportunity might not reappear for a long time.

It's wise, too, to remember that it's your positivity that's driving the energy of this card. Even though circumstances may have aligned to make this easier for you, it's still your own confidence and skills that are making this a sure bet. So believe in yourself, and send your creative arrows over the ramparts. Your ideas are good, they're hot, and they need to move with decisive strength *now.* Don't wait. NOW!

# NINE OF WANDS

KEYWORDS:
*Stamina*
*Strength*
*Capability*

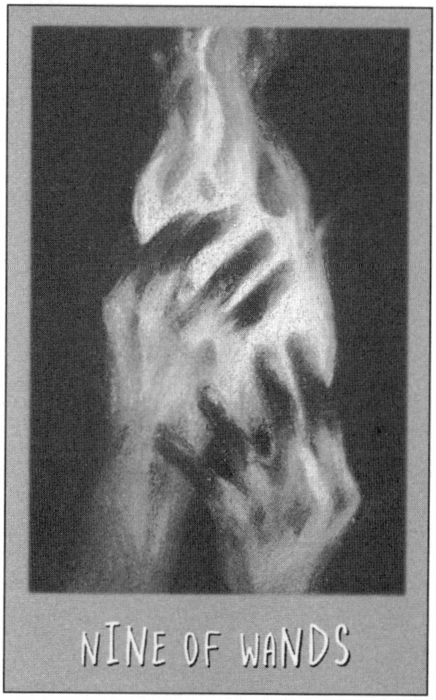


The Nine of Wands and Ten of Wands have always struck me as a bit of an odd way to end the suit of creativity—the Nine, in particular. The Nines of all the suits hover right on the edge of completion, increasingly following the theme of their given suit to its logical conclusion. But where the Nine of Coins and the Nine of Cups are exceptionally positive cards, and the Nine of Swords at least logically follows from the hardship of the rest of the swords suit, the Nine of Wands seems unfairly difficult for an otherwise productive suit. One might be tempted to live in the Nine of Coins or the Nine of Cups forever. But it would be pretty taxing to live in the Nine of Wands for a month, much less a lifetime.

It represents an effort that is nearly done, close enough to touch... except for one final push. And it's no minor obstacle that stands between you and completion. The final step is something that is going to test your inner strength to its utmost, something that depends on all of the experience and skill you've built up to this point.

The blackened fingers on the art show the experience won't be easy, but the confidence with which those blackened hands contain the fire speaks to how, at the very least, you have the skill to handle it. You can do it. It'll burn, but push through to success.

# TEN OF WANDS

KEYWORDS:
*Burden*
*Responsibility*
*Completion*

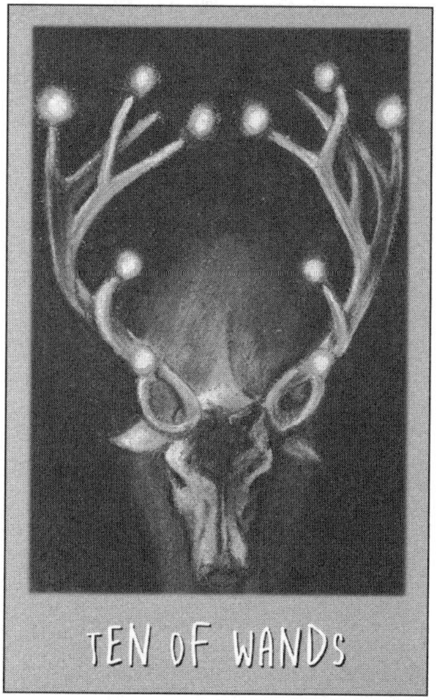


Well, that was tough.

When the Ten of Wands shows up, you've just worked hard to finish something, and now you find yourself looking at the results of that completion. Part of you is delighted; it's satisfying to be done, finally, to have finished something you set out to do. But part of you is weary. It was hard work, and now you realize that it's going to take even more work to maintain what you have. Celebration is the furthest thing from your mind.

The Ten of Wands might be urging you to seek help—more hands make for lighter labor, and in this case, maybe all you need to improve your life is another set of shoulders to help carry the weight of responsibility. It could also be reminding you that creativity is about beginnings and endings and then beginnings again. It can be hard to let go of something you've worked so hard on for so long, but this card can be a reminder that it's time to let go and start the cycle over again.

The elk on the card hangs its head with the weight of responsibility. It's strong enough to bear it, if that is what the elk chooses. But just a toss of its head could reignite the world with the fire still burning on its antler tips. When you see the Ten of Wands, you have to decide whether you need to maintain what you have made, or begin all over again.

# PAGE OF WANDS

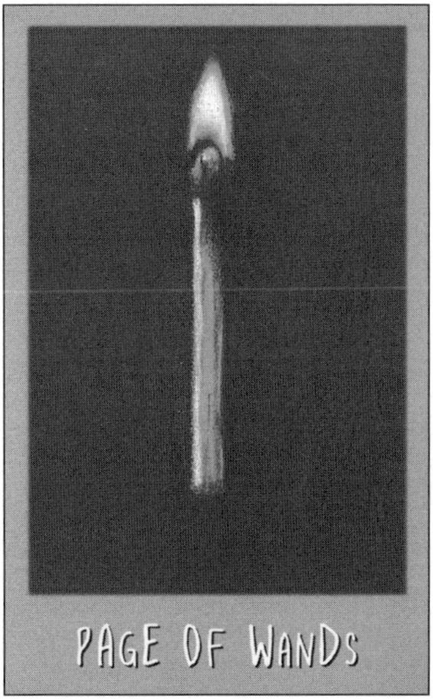


KEYWORDS:
*Spark*
*Curiosity*
*Confidence*

The Page of Wands is an enthusiastic firecracker of an individual, the living embodiment of the Ace of Wands. Courageous, she's childlike, confident, and undaunted by all of the things she has yet to learn in the world. The raw spark of an idea is enough to put her into motion. Practical concerns aren't even on the radar, or if they are, they are so vastly unimportant when compared to her singular interest in that new idea that they might as well be invisible.

When you find the Page of Wands in a spread, it might mean that you need to find that sort of fearlessness and spontaneity in you. Strip away the burdens and concerns that might keep you from pursuing an idea, and just let yourself be a creative visionary. Even if you know better than the Page, who has never had to encounter adversity, try to channel her youthful optimism.

The just-struck match on the card reminds you to act quickly. The Page is just the beginning; apply that fire to a bigger project before it goes out.

# KNIGHT OF WANDS

KEYWORDS:
*Energetic*
*Daring*
*Confident*
*Charming*

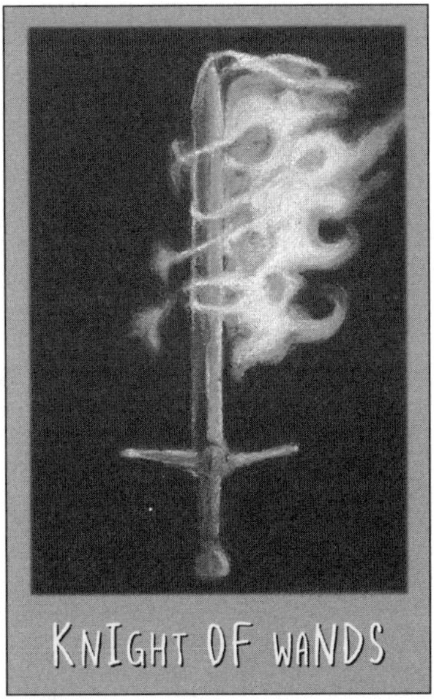


All of the Knights are fast movers, and the Knight of Wands is no exception. The Knight completely believes in herself and her interests, and as such, there is no doubt to slow her down. She barrels into situations with all guns blazing, pulling everyone's attention to her as only someone who is truly self-confident can. She has plenty of friends, because she is just as willing to blaze a righteous path of fury on someone else's behalf. It's easy to be bowled over by the Knight of Wands—you're not sure if you love or hate her as she overwhelms you with her daring and self-belief.

Sometimes when this card appears, it means you should try to channel that fearless speed of the Knight. With your beliefs firmly in tow, act now with a grin on your face and your hat cocked rakishly. Sometimes, however, it's a warning—the Knight can be a little too reckless, and sometimes rushing into a situation with nothing but charm and a promise will get you into trouble. Make sure the ground is solid beneath you before galloping over it.

The flaming sword on the card reminds you of all that can be accomplished with a powerful swing of a confident weapon. Remember to use the sword for others as well as yourself, because that's what keeps this Knight a hero.

# QUEEN OF WANDS

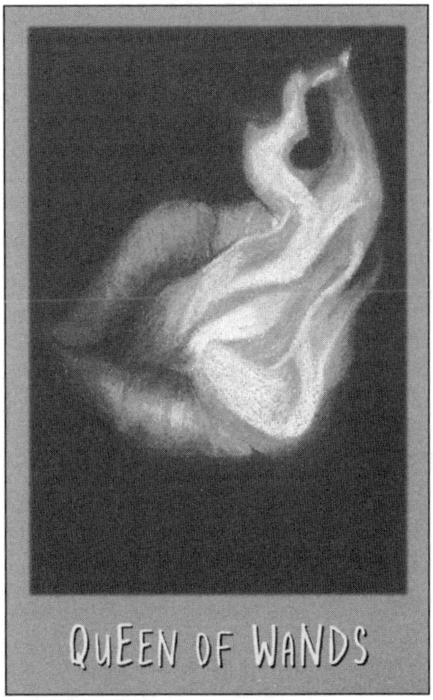


KEYWORDS:
*Creativity*
*Passion*
*Ferocity*
*Confidence*

The Queen of Wands breathes fire. She's powerful, ambitious, creative, and she's not afraid of all the challenges that come with those three things. She knows what she wants: the world. Although she can be stubborn—she knows what she wants, after all, and she's pretty sure she knows best how to get it—she attracts others to her because of her generosity of spirit. It can be appealing, too, to hand your problems over to her, because she will use her ferocity and passion to tackle them with the same energy as she tackles her own. In fact, she might take them from you against your will, because the Queen is so certain that she has the best solution to problems that it's difficult for her to let a bad situation fester without her interference.

This maternal protection is both the best and worst thing about the Queen of Wands. She's gifted at balancing her own ambitions with the needs of her brood, but she can also be overbearing and vicious when she feels her turf is being threatened. All of the wands make bad enemies, but the Queen finds it hard to let go.

When you see the Queen, it's a reminder that all of us are capable of breathing fire. Be certain that the situation *needs* your steam, and then blast away.

# KING OF WANDS

KEYWORDS:
*Inspiration*
*Ethics*
*Leadership*
*Boldness*

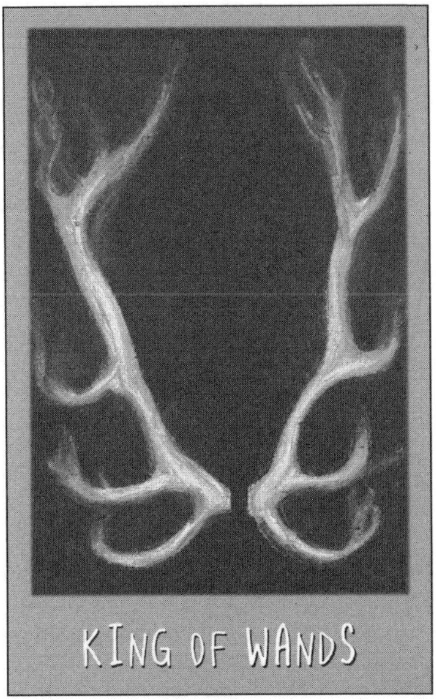


The King of Wands is much like the Ten of Wands. Both seem like they should epitomize the creativity suit, and yet, both of them have much more to do with responsibility than the actual act of creating. The King is the least actively creative of any of the wands court cards. Even though she's not making things herself, however, she is still deeply interested in creative people, and this is where her strength lies: in leadership. There's no one quite like the King of Wands for knowing how to bring out the best in other artists and idea-makers. That's good, because one thing a lot of creative types aren't gifted at is organization and delegation. The King is an *actual* king in this department. She can bring people together with a united idea and make them stronger as a whole than they were as individuals.

One of the King's faults, however, is that she always sees the best in people and the world; all of her ideas come from that place of fierce and ethical optimism. That doesn't seem like it should be a fault, but no one is flawless, and plans that rely on the perfection of all parties are destined to come up short. Remember to work for the ideal but be ready to accept the practical.

I chose fiery antlers for this card to echo the responsible sentiment of the Ten of Wands, but unlike the heavy antlers in the Ten, these are on fire with purpose. Hold your head high when you see this card, and lead the way.